WITHDRAWN

THE ORIGIN AND DEVELOPMENT
OF DRAMATIC CRITICISM
IN THE NEW YORK TIMES
1 8 5 1 – 1 8 8 0

John Rothman

ARNO PRESS
A Publishing and Library Service of The New York Times
NEW YORK
1970

Copyright © 1953 by John Rothman

Library of Congress Catalog Number 78-126346
ISBN 0-405-02560-2

Manufactured in the United States of America by
Arno Press, Inc., 1970

TABLE OF CONTENTS

PREFACE

The development of dramatic criticism in the daily newspapers appears to be a virgin field. The standard histories of journalism, and even the detailed histories of specific newspapers which have been published, deal with dramatic criticism only in passing, if at all; for them, it is only one function of a relatively minor department of the newspaper. The theatrical annals, and the numerous biographies and memoirs of actors, managers and other theatrical personages, use the dramatic reviews of the press as sources only, not as a subject of discussion *per se*; they seldom even identify any drama critic whom they quote by name, and, when they do, it is frequently for reasons other than his profession. The apparent neglect of this field is surprising, for the dramatic criticism of the newspapers, as a day-by-day chronicle of theatrical events and trends, seems certainly to be a valuable subject for study.

This study falls almost naturally into three parts. Part One contains chiefly a compilation of all available biographical material on the men who wrote, or who may have written, dramatic reviews for the New York Times between 1851 and 1880; it contains in addition some information on the critics of the Times as a group. This material has been collected in part from works on the newspapers, the theatre and the persons prominent on the stage during this period, and in part from scrapbooks and contemporaneous periodicals; most useful were the several memoirs of William Winter, and a speech of his which listed the names of some fifty drama critics of his day.[1]

Part Two is a detailed study of the reviews themselves, based on an examination of every single review published in the Times from the first issue, September 18, 1851, through September 30, 1857, and of every review published thereafter during two consecutive months of each year through 1879. For these twenty-two years, a different pair of months was selected each year to obtain the widest possible sampling. The two summer months, however, being off-season, were omitted throughout. Certain tangential material — ed-

---

1. *The Press and the Stage*, pp. 31, 44. Winter did not, however, identify the publications for which these critics worked.

itorials, feature articles and the like — has been included whenever
it seemed to be relevant, and some material on the critics' working
method, whatever could be discovered, was added.

Part Three consists of an attempt to identify the authors of given
reviews, as far as the available evidence and a reasonable amount of
speculation allow.

For the sake of simplicity, no distinction has been made between
the New York Times and the New York Daily Times, as it was
known before 1857; also, I have referred to it hereafter merely as
"Times," and have omitted the usual italics because of the frequency with which the word appears in this study. References
to it are made by year, month, day, page and column, in that order;
e.g., Times, 1851, Sept. 18, 1:1. Except for occasional references
to recent issues, the Times edition used has been the *Recordak
Micro-Film of the New York Times,* New York, The Recordak Cor-
poration. References to editorials or special supplements are so
marked. In quoting from the Times, special styles of printing, such
as small capital letters or bold-face type, have been ignored.

The Times was chosen in preference to other newspapers for various reasons, the most potent of which is probably that I, through
my employment by the Times, expected to have ready access to
whatever material its archives might contain. Actually, the Times
has no information on its dramatic critics of the period under study;
at least, none was available.[1]

It might be well to state at this point that I have made no
attempt to engage in — let alone solve — the age-old controversy
over the terms "critiques," "reviews" and "notices." "Critics"
and "reviewers," and "critiques" and "reviews" have been used
synonymously. The last two have been used in reference to articles, at least ten lines and usually two or more paragraphs in
length, which contain some analysis of the subject and express
opinions with a certain amount of detail. "Notices" refers to brief
mention of plays, seldom more than a five-line paragraph each and
resembling more an advertisement than an article.

I wish to express my sincere gratitude to the following persons
for their advice and guidance: Professors G. W. Allen and Albert S.
Borgman of New York University, Mr. Francis Brown of Time,
Inc., Mr. John Mason Brown, Mr. Barrett H. Clark, Mr. Herbert
Erb, Librarian of The Players, the Archivist of Harper Brothers &

---

1. Sulzberger, Arthur Hays, letter to John Rothman, Feb. 26, 1948.

Co., Professor Emory Holloway of Queens College, Mr. Carl T. Keppler of Steinway & Sons, Mr. William Letsch, Manager of the Lotos Club, Mr. Garrett Leverton of Samuel French, Inc., Mr. Montrose Moses, Jr., Professor George C. D. Odell, Professor Arthur H. Quinn of the University of Pennsylvania, Miss May Davenport Seymour of the Museum of the City of New York, Mr. William Van Lessep, Curator of the Theatre Collection of the Harvard College Library, and Professor Wolle of the University of Colorado.

I

THE REVIEWERS

Year after year the critics are denounced. Lean and hungry actors, licking their wounds at Sardi's after a miserable opening night, call them names and question the legal prearrangements for their birthdays. Producers . . . dictate fierce, but unsent, letters in which the words jackal and hyena predominate. Playwrights . . . cast their meter to the winds and, about the critics, revert to some of the terse phrases of Chaucer. The theatre, which seldom unites for any cause, always will join against the enemy. Damn them . . .

The charges against the critics are . . . blindness, lack of hearing and intoxication. . . . The critics know nothing, and they will not learn. . . .[1]

This in 1947.

. . . the great majority of those journalists who presume to print their estimates of histrionic performances are profoundly ignorant of the elements of the dramatic art . . . they victimize [the actors] . . . their cue is to depreciate and detract, to satirize and belittle, so as . . . to imply the superiority of their own knowledge and taste . . .[2]

This in 1877.

There has been some progress, nevertheless. In contrast to newspaper critics of our present age, those of the period from 1851 to about 1880 were charged not merely with negligence and ignorance, but with the most heinous crimes, ranging from personal animosity toward the actor or playwright who was the unfortunate target of a given review, to large-scale graft, bribery, and other forms of corruption, used at times to enrich the critic himself, at others to coerce some innocent theatre manager or publicity agent to avail himself of the advertising columns of a given newspaper.[3]

It seems too late now to pass judgment on these charges. Most certainly some were justified in some cases, if only on the basis of the where-there's-smoke adage. There is no record of a trial of this

1. Nichols, "The Nine Cold Men of Broadway," The New York Times Magazine, 1947, Nov. 16, 17:2.
2. Alger, Life of Edwin Forrest, II, 439.
3. Cf. Boucicault, "At the Goethe Society," (an address), North American Review, CXLVIII, 335; New York Dramatic News, Vol. III, Oct. 28, 1876, p. 5; The Round Table, Vol. I, Jan 2, 1864, pp. 43-44.

kind, concerning any newspaper, in the files of the Times; and there probably was never sufficient evidence to bring any case to trial. In view of the perennial animosity between the Times and the New York *Tribune*, to cite just one internal feud of the press, it is quite likely that one newspaper stimulated nasty rumors about the employee of a rival publication. On the other hand, it would be absurd to maintain that no unethical person ever entered the critics' profession; the Times itself may have had such an unethical critic in the person of Frederick Schwab. The charge of ignorance about the stage is equally hard to prove or refute about the critics of that day, since little relevant biographical material is extant. Still, of the dozen or more critics identified with the Times during the period under study, one became famous as a theatre manager, play adapter and translator, another, as a newspaper editor, a third, as a poet and short-story writer; two more were well-known feuilletonists and minor playwrights; and one is known to this day as an educator and textbook writer and editor. On the whole, they really form an impressive body of intellectuals, even if none of them is taught along with Aristotle in courses on criticism.

Professor Quinn writes that "I have never made an exhaustive study of dramatic critics' writings for newspapers because, as a matter of fact, I think very little guidance can be obtained from them."[1] Some objections may be raised to this. In dramatic literature, the third quarter of the last century was exceedingly barren, in America as well as in England; Bulwer-Lytton and Boucicault and possibly Tom Robertson are probably the best-remembered playwrights then living. But the theatre itself reached a new peak in achievement; Forrest, Booth, Jefferson and Rachel were only some of the top-notch actors who were then on the stage, a stage directed by such men as Wallack, Burton, Brougham and Daly. Of this, the living theatre, only three types of records remain: the playbills, the memoirs of theatrical personages, and the writings of the much-reviled newspaper critics; and of these, the newspaper reviews seem certainly the most comprehensive and informative. Subjective they are, to be sure; but it seems to me that they yield an invaluable store of data on individual performances of plays, on the minor plays, on staging and scenery, on acting and costumes, on audience reaction and on the general scope and quality of amusements in the city; and, finally, on such otherwise unrecorded incidentals as ben-

1. Letter to John Rothman, March 18, 1948.

efits, special events at theatre openings and at the beginning or the end of engagements, and the like.

With few exceptions, little is known of the lives of the critics then connected with the Times; and for those few, most available material pertains to activities outside their journalistic careers. In most cases, it has not even been possible to fix the exact dates of their employment as dramatic critics; and for some, no definite evidence connecting them with the Times, or proving that they wrote dramatic reviews for the Times, could be discovered. Available data point to Fitz-James O'Brien or Charles C. Bailey Seymour as having been the first to write dramatic critiques for the Times, unless, of course, there was someone of whom no record exists today; and the latest critic of the period covered appears to have been George Edgar Montgomery, who joined the Times in 1877. The following chart lists all persons who could be identified as having been critics during this period and who are known or are likely to have worked for the Times in this capacity.

New York Times Drama Critics
(1851 – 1879)

Reviewer	Year 1851 53 55 57 59 61 63 65 67 69 71 73 75 77 79
O'Brien	
Seymour	
W. Swinton	
Daly	
Schwab	
Montgomery	
Remack	
Wilkins	
Hurlbert	
Leland	
J. Swinton	
Fairbanks ⎫ Lancaster ⎬ Oakes ⎭	No precise identification possible

■■■ Definite evidence exists indicating employment as Drama Critic for the New York Times.

☐ Employment by the Times as drama critic is possible, but evidence is inconclusive.

Fitz-James O'Brien is probably the most colorful of the group, since he represents a combination of artistic genius with both vagabondism and a certain amount of beautiful heroism. He was born in Limerick, Ireland, in 1828,[1] and was educated at the University of Dublin. His family seems to have been well off financially, for he is said to have squandered a rather large inheritance within a few years in London. In 1851, he published a periodical during the International Exposition in London, and wrote several poems. He came to New York in 1852,[2] and started to work for several publications, including the Times, even though his main journalistic effort was devoted to the *Lantern*. He wrote at least five plays, collaborated on an unknown number of others, and wrote poetry and short stories, mostly for various periodicals and newspapers. Some of his poems appeared in the Times. His best-known literary work is probably his short story, *The Diamond Lens*. To the newspapers, he also contributed miscellaneous articles on art and literature—and, of course, dramatic reviews. Through his stormy friendship with Thomas Bailey Aldrich[3] and primarily through his association with Henry Clapp on the New York *Saturday Press*[4] he became a leader of the so-called Bohemian group that regularly met at Pfaff's restaurant to drink and dispute in the accepted style of Henri Murger's *Vie de Boheme*.[5] O'Brien early joined the Union Army in the Civil War, became a lieutenant, wrote a number of dispatches for newspapers from the front, and died in a Baltimore hospital on April 6th, 1862, after tetanus developed from a rather slight wound.[6]

The nature of O'Brien's relation to the Times is rather uncertain. "When the *Lantern* expired, O'Brien was tendered a position

1. This date is given by most authorities; but Greenslet says 1826.
2. Reilly puts it as early as 1848.
3. Greenslet, *The Life of Thomas Bailey Aldrich*, pp. 37-42.
4. Derby, *Fifty Years Among Authors, Books and Publishers*, p. 232.
5. For a brief description of this group, containing an apparently complete list of its members, see obituary of Henry Clapp, Times, 1875, Apr. 11, 7:3.
6. Obituary, Times, 1862, Apr. 10, 5:1; memorial article by William Sydney Hillyer, Times, Saturday Review of Books and Art, 1898, July 1, 445:1; Winter, introduction to *The Poems and Stories of Fitz-James O'Brien*, pp. xv-xxviii; Wolle, "Fitz-James O'Brien," *University of Colorado Studies*, Series B, Studies in the Humanities, Vol. II, No. 2. Professor Wolle's study is by far the most exhaustive. For additional material on O'Brien's biography and personality, cf. Arnold, an article from the New York *Citizen*, Sept. 30, 1865, reprinted in *The Poems and Stories of Fitz-James O'Brien*, pp. xlvii-liii; Fatout, "An Enchanted Titan," *South Atlantic Quarterly*, XXX, 51-59; Glicksberg, "Charles Godfrey Leland and 'Vanity Fair,' " *Pennsylvania Magazine*, LXII, 320-322; Parry, *Garrets and Pretenders*, pp. 32, 51; Reilly, "A Keltic Poe," *The Catholic World*, CX, 751-762; Winter, *Old Friends*, p. 67 ff.

as editorial writer on the Times, by Mr. Raymond, who appreciated his genius from the first.[1]   This indicates that O'Brien was a regular employee on the Times, and is supported by Derby's statement that O'Brien was an "assistant editor" of the Times by 1852.[2] Most other authorities, however, speak of a different kind of connection. Winter relates in his introduction to O'Brien's *Poems and Stories* that "He contributed, also, in a fitful and miscellaneous way, to . . . the *New York Times* . . ."[3]   The Times itself calls him "for many years a valued contributor."[4]   An obituary in *Harper's Weekly* speaks of his holding "recognized positions" on the Times and other publications,[5] but I think that this statement refers to his prestige rather than to a formal condition of employment. If he worked for the Times with any degree of regularity, it was certainly for a very short time only; for almost every single biographical sketch shows him as working only spasmodically — perhaps only when he could not sell anything free-lance, and when he was unable to borrow any money from his friends. A regular job, no matter how much prestige or money it involved, seems certainly incongruent with his character.

Whatever work he accomplished, however, seems to have found favor with his associates and with the reading and theatre-going public. Of his six plays, four were performed in New York in the 1850s, and at least one was revived after his death.[6] All were favorably reviewed in the Times. His poems — well, "he thought he was a poet . . . but a charitable posterity will leave his poems decently buried."[7] His weird, mysterious short stories are quite good; in fact, he has been called "the most distinguished American story-teller between Edgar Allen Poe and Bret Harte."[8] His main fault, according to his critics, was amazingly consistent with his character. "As a literary man, Lt. O'Brien was completely successful . . . but it was his whim to be fickle."[9] ". . . he was accepted . . . as . . . a clever writer . . . [but] there is no sincerity in his work.

---

1. Wood, letter to Winter quoted in *The Poems and Stories of Fitz-James O'Brien*, p. xxxix.
2. Derby, *op. cit.*, p. 354.
3. P. xvii.
4. Obituary, 1862, Apr. 10, 5:1.
5. Vol. VI., Apr. 26, 1862, p. 267.
6. Wolle, *op. cit.*, bibliography.
7. Edward James O'Brien, introduction to the *Collected Stories of Fitz-James O'Brien*, p. x.
8. *Ibid.*, p. viii.
9. Obituary, Times, 1862, Apr. 10, 5:1.

Haste is evident in all that he wrote, impatient carelessness and vio-
lated taste. We feel that he could have done better if he had taken
more pains, but he would not take the pains . . ."[1] All this seems
to indicate that he was as unruly an author as he was a man, and he
confirmed this himself when "he declared that he, as a grinder for
the morning journals, was sick of a dull uniformity . . ."[2] Except
for several poems, I have found only one signed piece of literary
work by him in the Times, an impassioned two-and-a-half column
article called "Art and Art Critics" and signed "F.J.O'B."[3] Even
though it treats only painting and sculpture, it is worth discussion
here because it shows that O'Brien belonged, body and soul, to the
romantic movement; and thus sheds, indirectly, some light on his
dramatic criticism which is otherwise totally obscure.

> There are a certain class of critics . . . [who] see nothing beyond
> forms, and their conceptions lie within the limits of a picture frame. They
> are technical and exoteric, and see all that is on the outside of a picture or
> a statue very distinctly. But of the long perspective of sentiment and
> feeling that stretches away behind the paint and canvas, or the divine
> thought that palpitates in the cryptical core of the marble, they are en-
> tirely oblivious.
>
> Those men have set up certain gods in the realm of Art.

Here follows a statement that most of the Old Masters, such as
Titian and Raphael, certainly were once considered great and still
are, but that their divinity has faded somewhat with the passage of
time.

> There is nothing so difficult to combat against as a name. Set a
> man's name in motion, and let it roll down the declivity of Time for
> five hundred years, and at the end of that period it will have acquired
> such . . . impetus that he is a daring man that will cross its path and cry
> 'stop!'

The rest of the article is devoted to an expansion of his thesis;
he criticizes the technical flaws in the Old Masters, asserts that the
Old Master worship tends to hinder the advancement of young

1. Stoddard, "The Best of the Bohemians," *The Critic*, Vol. I. Feb. 26, 1881, pp.
44-45.
2. Sherwood, (Mrs.) M. E. W., "Fitzjames [sic] O'Brien," Times Saturday Review of
Books and Art, 1898, July 2, 444:2.
3. 1852, Nov. 27, 3:1.

artists who are better than the "ancients" for their "poetic fidelity to Nature," and ends in a eulogy of Ruskin, the Pre-Raphaelites, and the Young American Artists.

O'Brien's dramatic criticism, as I said, is totally obscure, for none of it can be identified with any degree of certainty; but there are two general comments on it. Winter, in his introduction to the *Poems and Stories*, writes that O'Brien ". . . was possessed of a strong dramatic sense and had a good knowledge of the stage . . . and . . . could write with an incisive judgment and informing taste on the acted drama."[1] And Hillyer adds, in his obituary, that "He . . . was a firm believer in the natural school of acting, and advocated its theories when and where he could."[2] Finally, O'Brien the Drama Critic reveals himself in a review of Tennyson's *Maud and Other Poems*,[3] which is not signed but which Professor Wolle definitely assigns to him.[4] For, while the second and by far larger part of this article is devoted to the poetic aspects of *Maud*, his most scathing criticism concerns the fact that ". . . Mr. Tennyson has neither the clearness nor sequential faculty necessary to the development of dramatic action with a beginning, a middle and an end." He relates, O'Brien charges, events through the hero's reaction to them, "so that the reader gets at the result . . . before he learns the events themselves." This is unquestionably the language of an experienced drama critic.[5]

In several respects, O'Brien was totally different from his good friend Charles C. Bailey Seymour. Seymour's work for the Times was steady and regular; very little is known of his outside activities, or, in fact, of his entire biography; and, on the whole, he seems to have been a considerably more sober, staid and steady person than O'Brien. About his connection with the Times there is no doubt at all; his obituary in that newspaper states unequivocally that he "has been connected with the *Times* as its Musical and Dramatic Critic from nearly the beginning of its publication."[6] Winter reports that he started to work for the Times in 1855,[7] but since all other authorities leave the starting date blank, Winter's date

1. P. xix.
2. *Op. cit.*, 444:2.
3. Times, 1855, Nov. 13, 2:1.
4. *Op. cit.*, p. 108.
5. Some inconclusive evidence identifying O'Brien with certain reviews, and a discussion of the reviews presumed to be his, follow in Part III. Note that the same procedure has been followed for the other critics.
6. 1869, May 3, 5:1.
7. *Old Friends*, p. 311.

must be considered questionable.

Seymour was born on October 23, 1829, in London.[1] Nothing is known of his family background, his childhood or his education; all we know is that he came to New York in 1849, taught school for an undetermined length of time, and then joined the Times. From January to July, 1865, he was associated with Theodore Hagen in editing the New York *Weekly Review*, presumably on a leave-of-absence from the Times; and later during that same year he wrote a column called "Dramatic Feuilletons" for Clapps' New York *Saturday Press*, signed with the initials C. B. S.[2] Of course, he, too, belonged to the Bohemian circle. In 1858, he published a book called *Self-Made Men*, which consists of sixty-two biographical sketches of British, Scotch and American notables, varying from three to twenty-seven pages each and having no connection at all with the theatre. He also translated from the German two or three (unidentified) plays, and prepared them for stage presentation. In 1862, he covered the Great Exposition in London for the Times; and in 1867, he was appointed one of the American Commissioners for the Department of Music and Musical Instruments at the Great Exposition in Paris. He was in Paris, consequently, from April to September, 1868, and was decorated for his work by Louis Napoleon. While he was there, he married the sister-in-law of Mills, the pianist. Less than a year later, on May 2, 1869,[3] he died in his Union Square apartment of a malignant brain fever, from which he had been suffering, apparently, less than a week. He was survived by his widow, one child, and a brother who lived in Pittsburgh. On June 12, a memorial concert was given for him at Steinway Hall;[4] Steinway & Sons has no record of this concert beyond a brief mention in the diary of the late William Steinway that it was "but fairly attended."[5]

This appears to be all that is now known of the life of Seymour. I have found only one comment on his appearance: Lockridge describes him as "stately and . . . bearded."[6] But there is, fortu-

1. Winter says December 13, *ibid.*

2. These columns appeared irregularly. They consist of brief reviews of plays and of quips about theatrical personages and the audience. I found four in the issues of the *Saturday Press* available at the New York Public Library: 1865, Nov. 4, p. 216; Dec. 16, p. 312; Dec. 23, p. 328; Dec. 30, p. 344.

3. Winter says May 18 (*Old Friends*, p. 311), which would date Seymour's obituary fifteen days before his death. For that reason, Winter's dates appear to be unreliable.

4. Odell, *Annals of the New York Stage*, VIII, 522.

5. Letter to John Rothman, Nov. 20, 1947. For all the foregoing, see: obituary, Times, 1869, May 3, 5:1; *Appleton's Cyclopedia of American Biography*, 1900, V, 475; Winter, *Old Friends*, 311-313; Winter, *Brief Chronicles*, 258-260.

6. *Darling of Misfortune: Edwin Booth*, p. 114.

nately, considerably more material available on his work at the Times. The Times itself reports that "He was well known and very highly esteemed as a critic . . . being well-informed, conscientious and just. His style . . . was exceedingly clear, forcible and accurate . . . [He] contributed a good deal to other departments of literature, and always with ability and success."[1] Hillyer, in his obituary of O'Brien, calls Seymour the "Brilliant musical and dramatic critic of the New York Times."[2] Judge Daly lists him among the most prominent critics of the New York press in 1859.[3] Winter says that Seymour possessed all the necessary qualifications for a good critic, "learning, judgment, taste, sensibility, discernment, a kind heart and the habit of incessant industry . . . His incisive style was felicitous with lightness of touch . . . clear and terse. . ."[4]

Seymour's dispatches from Paris on the Exposition of 1868 throw little light on his career as a dramatic critic, numerous though they are. They contain a great deal of good-natured satire on the red tape, the exhibitors, the spectators and even the commissioners themselves, and, on the whole, present a good picture of the event.[5] But his lone article on the London Exposition of 1862 is highly relevant to his dramatic criticism, since, except for the opening paragraph, it does not treat the Exposition at all, but the state of the London stage of that date. "Some weeks ago, when I happened to be conversing with the manager of a theatre here, the potentate informed me that he had often thought of visiting New York just to show the good folks there how theatres *ought* to be managed." Seymour was not delighted with that prospect, since "Only a night or two previously I had visited this particular manager's theatre, had sat upon the hardest seat that can be found this side of purgatory, and had witnessed a play — produced according to said manager's idea of excellence." This idea pleased Seymour so little that he exclaimed: "*This* man to go to New York to show how to do things — to New York where there are gentlemen to manage theatres and artists to play in them!" And Seymour proceeded to "pan" this (never identified) London theatre with a vehemence bordering on viciousness — the scenery is patched, the carpets "simply infamous," the costumes "baggy, shiney [sic], shabby and ill-made."

1. Obituary, 1869, May 3, 5:1.
2. *Op. cit.*, 445:2.
3. *The Life of Augustin Daly*, p. 33.
4. *Old Friends*, p. 311.
5. 1868, Apr. 16, 1:2; Apr. 25, 1:5; subsequent articles appeared through August almost every week.

The best scene looked like a parlor in a fifth-rate boarding-house. . . .
And yet this theatre ranks with Mr. Wallack's, and can boast of one or
two distinguished artists, without counting the distinguished manager,
who, I believe, sometimes appears in a farce, or, worse still, writes one.
Conceive the fogginess of that manager's mind in believing for a moment
that what he does in this dingy hole of a theatre would be a revelation in
the bright little temples of America!

The English drama, Seymour continued, is in a dreadful state.
Young playwrights despair of ever finding a producer, because the
managers of first-class theatres are either playwrights themselves,
or collude with critics who write plays. And as to actors, most of
the successful plays in London star at least one touring American.
The appreciative audience is the best thing in "Those wretched
prisons called theatres; those dens of extortion; those hotbeds of
insolent rapacity; those conservatories of dust, darkness and dreari-
ness." "The fogies in London have all the theatres, the fogies in
London write in all the papers. There is a perfect understanding
between them. Nothing that is not fogy shall be tolerated. Hence
bad theatres, bad acting, bad plays, and the word 'good' for all."[1]
This article certainly justifies the attributes of "clear" and "terse"
and "forcible" which Winter applies to Seymour's style; it also
shows an amazing loyalty to his adopted country and very little
leniency toward his native England. It bears evidence – as much or
as little as a single article can – that the writer is deeply concerned
with theatrical developments, that he has an acute perception for
them, that he has the ability to present them lucidly, and that he
has a fine sense of humor in addition.[2]

What we know of Seymour, then, shows that the major portion
of his life was completely filled with the theatre and the concert
hall. For William Swinton, the exact opposite appears to have
been true: the writing of dramatic reviews was only a very minor
phase of his career. His brother John reports that he ". . . began
his newspaper career as a critic of the histrionic performances of
the great French actress, Mlle. Rachel, in New York. He knew
French well, and also the drama, and was selected to do this work

1. Times, 1862, Sept. 8, 2:1, 2.
2. It may be well to note here that Seymour is not the critic "lately come from England" who was charged by Joseph Jefferson with deliberately damning Forrest's performances in 1856 without having "scarcely seen a Shakespearean play." (*Autobiography of
Joseph Jefferson*, 167.) Not a single review of the Forrest performances appeared in
the Times in either 1855/1856 or 1856/1857.

for the *Times*.[1]   Since Rachel's only American tour took place in 1855,[2] John Swinton's statement places William on the Times in that year without any question. There is no evidence that he ever wrote any other dramatic reviews for the Times, or, in fact, for any other newspaper; nor is there any dubious period in his subsequent career during which he might have resumed his work as a drama critic. It seems therefore reasonable to conclude that he handled the Rachel performances as an unusual assignment, possibly because he was an able scholar rather than a professional drama critic.

Swinton was born in Salton, Scotland, on April 23, 1833, and in the twenty-two years before he joined the Times, he studied and taught at various colleges in Canada and the United States, married, had, for a short time, his own church as a Presbyterian minister, and contributed to *Putnam's Magazine*. The *Dictionary of American Biography* puts the date of his employment by the Times as late as 1858,[3] this, in view of his brother's statement, is certainly incorrect. Possibly, however, he worked for the Times on a part-time or free-lance basis only between 1855 and 1858. The Times itself does not indicate the date on which Swinton started to work for it.[4] During the Civil War, he was a war correspondent for the Times; his severe criticism of the Northern generals incurred him the enmity of General Grant and led, together with rumors of his obtaining information unethically, to the revocation of his correspondents' certificate in 1864. Thereafter, he remained a contributor to the Times for several years.[5] For the remainder of his life he wrote and edited the textbooks for history and philology courses for which he is still famous. He died on October 24, 1892.[6]

No other relevant material on William Swinton has been found.

The drama critic of the Times during that period who is today the most famous is undoubtedly Augustin Daly, who, following his newspaper career, became one of the foremost American theatrical producers of the seventies, second probably only to Lester Wallack. There seems to me to be little need to summarize here the bio-

1. Waters, *The Career and Conversation of John Swinton*, p. 27. For a discussion of the reviews, see Part Two.

2. Freedley and Reeves, *A History of the Theatre*, p. 312.

3. XVIII, 252.

4. Obituary, 1892, Oct. 26, 5:3.

5. Times, Jubilee Supplement, 1901, Sept. 18, 11:3 (issued Sept. 25).

6. Obituary, Times, 1892, Oct. 26, 5:3; *Dictionary of American Biography*, 1936, XVIII, 252.

graphical material on Daly;[1] it will suffice to present only those data which are relevant to his work for the Times. All available sources mention Daly as having written dramatic reviews for the Times for some time prior to 1869; they differ, however, on the length of the period during which he was so employed, and only too few make any critical comment on his work. In the *Memories of Daly's Theatres*, which was published during his lifetime and under his supervision, it is definitely stated that he was "dramatic critic on the New York *Times* from 1864 to 1868."[2] The biography by his brother, Judge Daly, leaves it vague: "For 10 years [1859-1869] he pursued this calling, and earned such a reputation for honesty that he gradually came to be employed at the same time as dramatic critic on the *Sun*, the *Express*, the *Citizen*, and the *Times* . . ."[3] Two different articles in the Times contradict each other: his obituary reports that he contributed to the Times "for a few months,"[4] while the Jubilee Supplement of 1901 states that he was, ". . . for a year or two, before the death of Mr. Raymond [June 17, 1869], the dramatic critic of the Times."[5] Winter, finally, says that he became drama critic on the Times in 1867.[6] Judge Daly's statement probably does not mean that he worked on the Times for ten years, but that his entire journalistic career lasted that long. Even when this statement is ignored, however, the period for Daly's connection with the Times still varies from four years to a few months, and there seems to be no solution for this problem now. It is quite likely that he wrote for the Times as well as for several other publications during the Civil War, since most of them were short-staffed, but his work for the Times may then have been so irregular as to be insignificant. From 1867 to 1869 he probably wrote for the Times more frequently, since all the sources cited place him with the Times then; he probably substituted for Seymour, who, it must be remembered, was in Paris for the Exposition during the spring and summer of 1868. Seymour's appointment came during 1867, and it is quite possible that he was so busy with the preparations for the Exposition that he was unable to

1. Consulted were: Daly, *op. cit.*, Hall, "Personal Recollections of Augustin Daly," *The Theatre*, V, 150-153, 174-175, 188-191, 213-215; scrapbooks and clipping files at the New York Public Library, the New York Historical Society and the theatre library of the Museum of the City of New York.
2. P. 17.
3. P. 33.
4. 1899, June 8, 2:1.
5. Sept. 18, 11:3.
6. *The Wallet of Time*, I, 349.

work for the Times regularly in that year. It is significant in that connection that none of the regular or doubtful critics other than Daly or Seymour are identified with the Times during those two years; so that, barring the existence of a critic entirely unknown, Daly appears to be the logical substitute for Seymour at that time. He may have retained the position until 1869 when he retired from the press altogether.

No signed articles by Daly were found in the Times; and the comment on his work is indeed scant. The Times notes that "... journalism ... was to him but a stepping stone to theatre management."[1] Judge Daly is equally brief: "His work was praised by Henry J. Raymond..."[2] Winter says that his "... criticisms ... were notable for direct, explicit, piquant statement of opinion, often condemnatory ..." and that they had "spontaneous, unaffected, complete disregard for established reputations."[3] (This is probably what Judge Daly meant by his "reputation for honesty.") The New York *Dramatic News* offers this rather caustic comment: "Mr. Daly ... was a journalist and a very bad one ... From the very fact, however, that he was a failure on the newspapers, he has been successful on the stage."[4] No other biographer, critic or theatre historian has apparently uncovered any further material on this phase of Daly's life; this is to be regretted, since a decade of dramatic criticism probably helped to shape Daly's subsequent work as playwright, play adapter and theatre manager.

From the time that Daly quit newspaper work to manage his own theatres, in 1869, to about 1872 there is a complete blank. Reviews, of course, continued to appear in the Times with the same frequency as before; but it has been impossible to identify their author (or authors) during these three years. The critic who emerges from this interregnum is Frederick A. Schwab (or Swab), whose career seems to have been an exceedingly curious mixture of fame and notoriety. His extant biography is very meagre indeed. He was born in 1844, undoubtedly of German or Austrian parentage, translated two French plays into English (Meilhac and Halevy's "Frou-Frou" and Scribe's "Adrienne Lecouvreur"), and "... served as music critic of the New York Times from about 1875 until about

1. Editorial, 1899, June 9, 6:1.
2. *Op. cit.*, p. 43.
3. *Vagrant Memories*, p. 220.
4. Vol. III, No. 6, 1876, Nov. 4, 4:2.

1890." Shortly thereafter he went abroad, and did not return to the United States. He died in Paris on June 10, 1927. "As an authority on music and the theatre for the Times . . . Schwab was a well-known figure in New York in the seventies, eighties and nineties . . . he was a man of great wit and charm . . ."[1] Apparently, he had joined the Times some years before 1875, however, for the *Courier des Etats-Unis* of September 9, 1872, already mentions him as "critique musicale du New York Times." He was a charter member of the Lotos Club, founded in 1870 as a social organization for journalists, critics, actors and artists, and was elected vice-president at its organization meeting.[2] He was not listed as an officer in 1873,[3] but was again elected vice-president in 1876.[4] In 1895 he is no longer even listed as a member,[5] probably because he was already abroad. There is no other information about Schwab in the club's records. He apparently spoke French fluently; this is evident not only from his translation of the two plays, but also from the fact that when he presided at a Lotos Club reception for Jacques Offenbach, he "first addressed the Club in English, . . . then turned to M. Offenbach, and speaking in French, welcomed him to the United States."[6]

All other extant information on Schwab comes from a single source — the New York *Dramatic News* — and is consistently unfavorable. The very first issue says that "The musical critic of the *New York Times* appears at times to be very much of an ass . . ." and charges that he would not have committed a certain error in one of his reviews if he had known his business.[7] The next issue hints that Schwab is not only stupid, but unethical:

> With the *New York Times*, the most respectable of our dailies, dramatic criticism should be a prominent feature, and we do not suppose the length of the advertisements has much to do with the tone of the notices. Unfortunately, the critic himself is not above suspicion. He does private writing of advertisements . . . and so on for some of our managers, and is paid for the work. He should naturally not speak harshly of those who employ him.[8]

1. Obituary, Times, 1927, June 11, 19:4.
2. Elderkin, *A Brief History of the Lotos Club*, I, 9.
3. *Ibid.*, p. 23.
4. *Ibid.*, II., 4.
5. *Ibid.*, pp. 49, 57.
6. Times, 1876, May 7, 7:2.
7. 1875, Oct. 2, 4:4.
8. Oct. 9, 4:1.

Two weeks later, this critic is identified as "Mr. Schwab," and is said to have been greatly embarrassed by this criticism.[1] In the following issue, the Town Crier column of the *Dramatic News* announces that ". . . Mr. Schwab, the gentleman who writes the musical and dramatic notices in the *Times*, is about to retire from that lucrative position, whether forcibly or voluntarily, has not transpired. I conceive it must be forcibly . . ."[2] On November 13, the same columnist viciously satirizes him in a mock dialogue between a publisher and a citizen, and reports that Schwab is about to lose his position as business agent for the actress Adelaide Neilson, after resigning his twenty-five-dollar-a-week job on the Times, and is now trying to recover this post.[3] Then the "Town Crier" tends to other affairs for about six weeks, and returns to Schwab only on December 25, reporting that Schwab, apparently still (or again) on the Times, attacked C. J. Smith's "The Flatterer" to avenge a slight he received at a party given by Smith on the opening night of the play. The same column notes that Schwab wrote two plays himself, "The Life and Times of Richard III" and "The Phantom King"; and sarcastically refers to the fact that the first ran for one night, and the second for two nights.[4] A month later, the ouster of manager Hart Jackson from the Brooklyn Theatre is discussed, with a note that ". . . the pimple in the trouble appears to have been that little Franco-German-composite excrescence – Swab."[5]

Until August, there appears only one brief note that "that little repulsive fellow Swab is now in Europe . . ."[6] But on August 12, the columnist, apparently incensed by Schwab's re-election as vice-president of the Lotos Club, threatens an exposé: "The facts I shall lay before the public . . . as to his bribery by managers for the use of his pen in the dramatic columns of the *Times*, will, I hope, cause . . . his being kicked out of the Club. Then, if the *Times* can stand him, so much the worse for the *Times*."[7] Something, however, must have deterred the writer from carrying out his threat. Considerably later, the *Dramatic News* published a charge that Schwab declined to see a performance by Augusta Dargon in Brooklyn without a "personal invitation" from the star, allegedly because he

1. Oct. 23, 4:3.
2. Oct. 30, 4:4.
3. 5:1.
4. 4:4.
5. 1876, Jan. 22, 4:4.
6. 1876, July 22, 5:1.
7. 5:1, 2.

did not receive an expected bribe.[1]   On October 23, the whole
column is devoted to Schwab's alleged partiality to Adelaide Neilson, with some veiled references to his business connections with
her.[2]   From February 17, 1877, on, the attacks are published
almost weekly; the series starts with a statement that "we have the
allegation of a manager that this gentleman [Schwab] was on his
regular payroll . . ."[3]   For the next two weeks, the columnist discusses the rumor that Schwab may marry Adelaide Neilson, express-
ing amazement that she could lower herself to contemplating an
alliance with such a creature, openly advising her against it, and
hinting that Schwab is using his position on the Times and his connections in the theatre world to blackmail her into the marriage so
that he can get her considerable fortune.[4]   On March 24, he
writes that ". . . Adelaide Neilson was puffed . . . to the exclusion
of others by little Swab, until Mr. George Jones . . . [realized] that
this venal little thing was directly interested in Miss Neilson's business affairs.   Then he put a stop to it."[5]   In the next issue, the
London *Figaro* is cited as deploring Miss Neilson's marriage plans.[6]
On April 7, the columnist reports that the marriage plans have been
abandoned, and immediately resumes the attack on Schwab from
a new angle — it had apparently been rumored that the Lotos Club
was about to dissolve, and the club's failure was blamed on Schwab's
alleged misconduct in office.[7]   In the next issue, Schwab is reported to have reviewed Miss Dickinson's play "The Crown of
Thorns" in full even though he rushed out after the first act.[8]

Then, after almost a half year of silence, the attacks reach their
climax with a report that the managers of the New York theatres
held a conference on plans to drive Schwab out of the critic's profession.   Only the opposition of two managers, the columnist reports, prevented the conference from adopting a plan whereby
representatives would tell Mr. Jones that all the theatres would
withhold their advertising from the Times unless Schwab was dis-
missed.   (The two opponents of this plan reportedly objected on
the grounds that such a move would constitute blackmail.)[9]

1. Oct. 7, 5:1.
2. 5:3.
3. 4:3.
4. Feb. 24, 4:4; March 3, 4:3, 11:2.
5. March 24, 9:1. Jones was then the publisher of the Times.
6. 4:3.
7. 4:3.
8. 4:2.
9. Sept. 22, 5:1.

Apparently nothing came of the managers' scheme, at least at
that time, for the *Dramatic News* does not even mention Schwab
again until over five months later, when the "Town Crier" reports
the weekly salaries of the New York dramatic critics as follows:

F. De Fontaine, New York *Herald*,	$40.—
Frederick Schwab, New York *Times*,	$35.—
William Winter, New York *Tribune*,	$25.—
A. C. Wheeler, New York *Sun*,	$35.—
Mr. Copleston, New York *World*,	$35.—
Mr. Davey, New York *Spirit*,	$30.—
Mr. Howes, New York *Express*,	$15.—
Mr. Towle, New York *Post*,	$25.—
Col. Atkinson, New York *News*	$25.—
Mr. Sigel, New York *Staats-Zeitung*,	$12.—
Mr. Ashley, New York *Clipper*,	$22.—

Schwab's salary is now given at $35.—, or ten dollars more than in
November, 1875 — a rather surprising increase for less than two
and a-half years. What is even more surprising is the "Town Crier's"
comment on this tabulation: ". . . by this exposure I only wish to
point a moral. A great deal has been said of the venality of the
New York Critics. Is it any wonder?"[1] Evidently he ascribes the
alleged corruption of the critics to the low compensation they received for their work, if, indeed, this compensation could be considered low for the 1870s.

Two and a-half months later, the *Dramatic News* reports that
Schwab has been discharged as dramatic editor of the Times, deplores the fact that this move has come so late, and thus reviews
all the charges that have been brought against him:

> . . . While a critic, he has been openly accused of being on the pay-
> rolls of several metropolitan theatres, and it caused no small speculation
> that Mr. Jones was aware of these facts and did not discharge him before.
> Beyond this, it was a matter of notoriety that, while a critic, Mr. Swab
> acted as the agent here of Adelaide Neilson, and received pay for the
> same. He also made several attempts to write plays, and used his posi-
> tion to get them accepted. In several cases they were accepted and met
> with direst disaster. He did not hesitate to take money from managers at
> every available opportunity, ostensibly for work done, but in reality to
> purchase his favorable opinion. In fact by his public and private acts he
> brought dishonor on his calling. I have on various occasions shown the
> venality and hardihood of the man, and have put backbone into some of
> those managers, who fearing his displeasure, dared not make their com-
> plaints to the fountain head. That Mr. Jones so often disregarded these

1. 1878, March 2, 4:4.

warnings almost convinced me that he dared not part with Swab. But
it is a long lane that has no turning, and at last the head of the critical
viper has been officially trod upon. Very few will regret his downfall
and many will justly rejoice. . . . We may indeed henceforth look on Mr.
Swab as a dead cock in the pit. Now let us have a critic on the *Times*
who shall, in character and attainments, be worthy of the standing of
that paper.[1]

For the remainder of the period under study, there are few
references to Schwab. One, on June 15, 1878, quotes the expense
account of the Ahrens Pappenheim Opera Company, printed in the
New York *Sun*, and hints that an item of one hundred dollars paid
to "Sch." constitutes a bribe to Schwab.[2] Subsequent references
merely note the "fall" of Schwab, without going into any further
details.[3]

On the whole, it is rather difficult to properly evaluate this material. Against the *Dramatic News'* report that Schwab was discharged from the Times in 1878 stands the Times' report that he
was employed by the Times until about 1890; and the only way to
reconcile these statements is by supposing that Schwab served in a
capacity other than that of dramatic critic after 1878. This is a
likely conclusion, even though there is no supporting evidence; presumably, he continued to write the musical criticisms. But why, if
the charges against Schwab were true, would the Times have continued to employ him for over a decade following his reported discharge as dramatic critic? And would the Times have praised him
so highly in the obituary if there had been such a scandal connected
with his work for the Times?

And there are other factors which indicate that the charges in the
Dramatic News cannot be taken for gospel truths. It appears that
in the Times' reviews of the seasons of 1875-1876, 1876-1877, and
1877-1878, Adelaide Neilson is seldom mentioned, and while she
is praised, it is never with such effusiveness as the *Dramatic News*
suggests. Certainly there are entirely too few reviews of her performances to warrant the extensive attacks on that score. (Nor is
there any reason to believe that the *Dramatic News'* columnist referred to any reviews by Schwab other than those in the Times.)
The alleged affair with Miss Neilson is mentioned nowhere else, and
she was famous enough as an actress and as a beautiful woman that
such a scandal would have found its way into other publications.
Certainly her divorce from Phillip Lee caused enough of an uproar

1. 1878, May 25, 4:5.   2. 4:2.
3. *passim*.

in the press of New York as well of London. She was also, indeed, a very great actress — she is said to have been the greatest Juliet of all time — so that all mention of her is laudatory as a matter of course, and does not necessarily indicate any corruption of the critic.[1]

There are still other points which make the attack on Schwab appear implausible. There is nothing to indicate that the two specific reviews which the *Dramatic News* assails were biased or even unusually malicious. The article on "The Flatterer"[2] praises the theatre, the production and the acting, but considers the play itself a failure, and suggests a certain sadness on Schwab's part that the new manager should have started his venture so inauspiciously. "The Crown of Thorns" was a revival; Schwab's review[3] implies that he had seen the original performance in Boston some eleven months earlier, and that he was convinced within a very short time that there had been no substantial changes in the production. It is impossible to tell from the review whether or not Schwab left after the first act; but his opinion of this as well as of the other play seems to have concurred with the consensus of the New York critics.[4]

At the same time, there are certain factors which tend to support the charges in the *Dramatic News*. The Times published no denial of the charges at any time, nor is there any record of any action Schwab may have taken to refute the charges, either in the press or in court. This is extremely suspicious, since a man in Schwab's position would have almost been forced to institute libel action if the charges had been untrue. It is even more suspicious because the Times always had a kind of predilection for publishing, and frequently participating in, controversies among theatrical people; for example, the editors themselves waged a war with Dion Boucicault in November and December of 1853 over charges of plagiarism in his play "The Fox Hunt" — a war that occupied the editorial page

1. To check Schwab's connection with Miss Neilson, the following works were consulted: *Appleton's Cyclopedia of American Biography*, 1900, IV, 488; Bodeen, "Adelaide Neilson of the Midnight Eye," *Pasadena (California) Playhouse News*, June 15, 1936, p. 4; "Adelaide Neilson," *New York Clipper*, LVII, 502; obituary, Times, 1880, Aug. 16, 7:3; Holloway, *Adelaide Neilson, A Souvenir*; Odell, *op. cit.*, IX and X, *passim*; Winter, *Wallet of Time*, I, 544-561; New York Public Library, clipping folders and scrapbooks on Adelaide Neilson from the Robinson Locke and Steed Collections.

2. Times, 1875, Dec. 14, 4:6.

3. Times, 1877, Apr. 5, 5:2. A review of the Boston performance, possibly written by Schwab, appeared in the Times, 1876, May 9, 7:1.

4. Odell, *op. cit.*, X, 100, 261-262.

almost every day for more than two weeks. In addition, there is
the great scarcity of material on Schwab in the Lotos Club; it seems
more than strange that there are virtually no records there on the
club's first vice-president, especially since he died relatively recently
and was, at the time of his death, the last charter member. Then
there is the unexplained trip to Europe when Schwab was already
close to fifty years old, and his failure to return to the United
States for the remaining thirty-odd years of his life.

Finally, there is the incontrovertible fact that, about 1877, the
Times did hire someone else to serve as drama critic — George Edgar
Montgomery — and that Schwab was probably not employed as a
drama critic thereafter. Thus it appears, while many of the detailed
allegations against Schwab may be based on gossip and rumor, there
is some measure of truth behind them; it is impossible, however, to
reach any more definite conclusions at this time.

The hiring of Montgomery by the Times was, of course, reported
by the *Dramatic News*: "The New York *Times* has lately committed its department of dramatic criticism to Mr. George Edgar Montgomery . . ." He has been writing poetry, the columnist continues,
poetry which was so bad that the Times' readers finally wrote to
Jones and asked that Montgomery be transferred to another department. "Mr. Jones acted on their request, and, remembering that in
little Fweddie [*sic*] Swab's time the department of the *Times* least
read was its dramatic column, thoughtfully ordered it to be turned
over to Mr. Montgomery . . ."[1]   Montgomery's obituary in the
New York *Dramatic Mirror* states that he was born about 1858,
was educated in Paris, returned to New York in 1877, became a
drama critic on the Times in that year, and held that position until
1884. Subsequently, he wrote poetry, and in 1886 became an as-
sociate editor of *The Theatre*. He died on August 22, 1898.[2]
The obituary in the Times adds only that some of his poems were
published in *Harper's Weekly*.[3]

Montgomery published, in 1890, a booklet on the public recitals
of Sidney Woollett; in the introduction, he refers to a review of
Woollett's recital of "Macbeth" which he (Montgomery) wrote for
the Times in 1880.[4] The *Dramatic News*, in its first mention of
Montgomery quoted above, condemned his review of "Otto, the

1. 1878, Nov. 9, 11:2.
2. Vol. XXXIX, 1898, Sept. 3, 13:3.
3. 1898, Aug. 24, 7:6.
4. *Sidney Woollett*, p. 4.

German" as inconsistent "twaddle," with a severity that almost
equalled its criticism of Schwab. Apparently taken to task for this
article, the *Dramatic News* published an editorial in which it de-
fended its criticism of Montgomery's review, but added in no uncertain terms: "We know Mr. Montgomery to be cultured and educated. We believe him to be inflexibly honest . . ."[1] Once more,
during the period under study, does the *Dramatic News* refer to
Montgomery. This time, it points out that two of his reviews of
Cazauran's "Lost Children," which appeared in the Times about
two months apart, are completely contradictory; but again it has-
tens to add that "Mr. George Edgar Montgomery, of the *Times* . . .
shares with Mr. Copleston, of the *World*, the credit of writing the
only unbiased and fairly impartial daily-press criticism in this city
. . ."[2]

The only other material available on Montgomery comes, curi-
ously enough, from no less a source than Walt Whitman. Traubel
reports Whitman as saying, on May 16, 1888:

'I have met George Edgar Montgomery, a young man who originally
promised much: who went to *The Times*, became dramatic critic —
worked hard, hard like a slave. He is, perhaps, another fine spirit destined for sacrifice — destined to the grind, the terrific strain, incident
to metropolitan journalism.'[3]

A letter to Whitman from William D. O'Connor, dated July 12,
1883, gives the following additional data on Montgomery:

'I wrote to Montgomery by way of attaching him, and had a very
cordial and friendly reply. He has lots of talent, but a vicious way of
temporizing — qualifying his statements — which he ought to get over.
His letter, too, gave me an unpleasant impression of pertness and con-
ceit. I fear he is an uneradicable sophomore, but he is friendly to us and
we need friends.'[4]

Montgomery is referred to only once more in Traubel's work, in
H. Johnston's letter to Whitman, dated March 25, 1884: " 'Mr.
Montgomery was wonderfully delighted with meeting you, and
talked on nothing else all day and evening. He is a man of very
marked ability, who will be heard of before long in politics and
literature. I think he has a wonderfully well-balanced mind.' "[5]
His prediction evidently did not come true; absolutely no further
data on Montgomery have come to light. This is deplorable, since
it is apparent from the two letters that Whitman and his friends

1. 1878, Nov. 16, 6:2   2. 1879, June 7, 8:2.
3. *With Walt Whitman in Camden*, I, 165.   4. *Ibid.*, III, 130.
5. *Ibid.*, p. 331.

tried to attach Montgomery to the pro-Whitman circle; I believe
that O'Connor's statement — "he is friendly to us and we need
friends" — leads to only one conclusion, namely, that Montgomery
was approached to write favorable reviews of Whitman's works,
and that he was apparently willing to comply. The whole matter
is, of course, only tangential to Montgomery's career as a drama
critic of the Times, but since so little is known about him, it appeared useful to include this information here.[1]

About half of Montgomery's career on the Times, and the larger
part of Schwab's, post-date 1879 and are thus outside the scope of
this work. There remain for discussion, however, some eight men
whose connection with the Times is rather uncertain, and who have
to be included here only because there is no evidence to prove that
they were *not* drama critics of the Times.

Of these, Edmund Remack probably was, chronologically, the
first. The fact that he was a drama critic was established by Winter;[2] and it is just barely possible that he contributed dramatic
reviews to the Times. His obituary in the Times refers to him as
"…a distinguished journalist, editorially connected with the *Abend-
Zeitung* of this City … [and] a highly appreciated contributor to
several prominent papers of this country and Europe."[3] To substantiate the assumption that the Times was one of these "prominent papers," there is only one, admittedly highly unreliable, piece
of evidence: a review, in the Times of October 20, 1852, of "Jack
Cade," signed with the initial "R."[4] Remack appears to be the
only drama critic then living in New York whose name starts with
the letter "R."

Almost nothing is known of his life. The obituary in the Times
confines itself to some vague generalities, and, following his death,
the Times only notes plans for a memorial concert for Remack.[5]
Remack's only extant work is a translation from German into English of Professor Hermann Zopff's *Practical Advice for Singers*.

For Edward G. P. Wilkins, even unreliable evidence is lacking.
It is known that he was a journalist, and probably a drama critic,

---

1. No further mention of Montgomery was found in any of the Whitman biographies,
his *Collected Prose*, or the manuscripts in the Berg Collection of the New York Public
Library. Nor could any material on him be uncovered in personal consultation with Professors Emory Holloway and G.W. Allen.
2. *The Press and the Stage*, p. 31.
3. 1868, Nov. 6, 5:1.
4. 2:5.
5. 1868, Nov. 10, 4:6; Nov. 19, 4:6; Nov. 21, 5:2.

in New York prior to 1857, and since he cannot be identified with any specific publication, it is possible that he was then writing for the Times. Wilkins was one of the earliest and most prominent members of the Bohemian circle. He had been a journalist in New York for some years prior to 1857; in that year, he wrote a regular column called "Bohemian Walks and Talks" for *Harper's Weekly* under the pseudonym "Bohemien." The last of these columns appeared on April 3, 1858. For about one year, then, he worked for Henry Clapp on the *Saturday Press*, under the pseudonym "Personne," and subsequently became a drama critic on the New York *Herald*. He held this position until his death in 1861, and is said to have been the most famous critic of his day, with the possible exception of Andrew Carpenter Wheeler. Nothing else is known of him, except that he wrote two comedies, which were published and performed, with moderate success, in 1856: "Young New York" and "My Wife's Mirror."[1]

William Henry Hurlbert was definitely a drama critic, and was for several years definitely employed by the Times; but whether or not he ever wrote drama reviews for the Times is uncertain. In fact, there is very little about him that can be asserted with any degree of certainty — even the spelling of his name varies from Hurlbert to Hurlburt to Hurlbut. (He is said to have preferred the first spelling.) He was born in Charleston, South Carolina; the date of his birth is variously given as July 3, 1827, July 13, 1827, and 1828. He spent his youth between study, mostly at Harvard University, and travel, until, in 1855, he joined *Putnam's Monthly* for several months, and subsequently became drama critic of the *Albion*. "In the Spring of 1857, Henry J. Raymond made him an offer to join the New York *Times*, which he accepted . . ." The position offered him was apparently that of editorial writer, and it is quite possible that, as such, he wrote dramatic reviews.[2]

In 1858, he went to Europe, probably to cover the Austro-Italian wars for the Times; a dispatch on the war in 1859 is ascribed to him.[3] In 1858, also, he wrote a play, "Americans in Paris."[4]

1. Arnold, "Edward Wilkins," *The Poems and Stories of Fitz-James O'Brien*, pp. xlvi-liii; Derby, '*op. cit.*, p. 232; *Harper's Weekly*, I, 707 to II, 211, *passim*; Ireland, *Records of the New York Stage*, II, 664; Parry, *op. cit.*, pp. 24, 32, 50, 56; Henry Clapp obituary, Times, 1875, Apr. 11, 7:3; Winter, *Old Friends*, pp. 84-88.
2. *Dictionary of American Biography*, IX, 424; Evans, "William Henry Hurlbert," Times Saturday Supplement, 1902, June 14, 1:1.
3. Mitchell, *Memoirs of an Editor*, p. 220.
4. Quinn, *The American Drama from the Civil War to the Present Day*, I, 39. The play was revived at Wallack's in 1871 (Times, May 5, 5:2).

He returned to New York in 1861, and became a war correspondent for the Times; his letters from the front were published in the
Times at irregular intervals.[1] In 1861, he was arrested in Rich-
mond, escaped the following year, and continued to write for the
Times until a rift over national politics caused him to change to the
New York *World*, in 1862. From then on until 1883, with the exception of three years on the *Commercial Advertiser* (1864-1867),
he stayed on the *World*; for the last seven years of that period he
was its editor-in-chief. In 1884 he went to Europe, where he remained until he died in September, 1895.[2]

Except for the Civil War dispatches, Hurlbert's writings for the
Times could not be identified. However, in view of the fact that
he wrote at least one play, was listed by Winter among the outstanding drama critics of the period,[3] and was the drama critic of the
Albion for probably one year, it is likely that he wrote some dramatic reviews for the Times. There is little comment on his work
and personality extant. The *Dictionary of American Biography*
calls him a "Brilliant but erratic genius," and notes that he "could
work on two or three editorials at once . . ." Charles Godfrey
Leland described him as handsome and passionate, but with "a
screw loose somewhere," and notes that the New York *Herald*
habitually referred to him as "The Reverend Mephistopheles Hurlbut."[4] Certainly his scholastic record and his eminent position
on the *World* corroborate the assumption that Hurlburt was a man
of outstanding abilities.

Leland had good reason to know Hurlbert, for he was asked to
substitute for Hurlbert until a permanent replacement could be
found. This permanent replacement, a "Mr. Hammond," was apparently supposed to start working for the Times within six months
after Hurlbert left for Italy, in 1858; but for some unknown reason
he never filled the position, and Leland stayed on until Hurlbert returned in 1861. Leland is too well-known to warrant a detailed
discussion of his biography; the only phase of it that need concern
us here is his three years' connection with the Times. He said that
he filled Hurlbert's place as "editorial writer"; if it is possible that
Hurlbert then wrote dramatic reviews for the Times, the same pos-

1. 1862, Sept. 11, 1:6; Oct. 11, 2:1; 20, 2:1; 30, 2:1.
2. *Dictionary of American Biography*, IX, 424; Evans, *op. cit.*; Mott, *American Journalism,* pp, 339, 434; obituary, Times, 1895, Sept. 7, 8:6.
3. *The Press and the Stage,* p. 31.
4. *Memoirs,* II, 17.

sibility must be admitted for Leland. Leland himself corroborated the assumption when he reported that Henry Raymond told him that ". . . now and then, whenever he wanted a really superior art criticism, I should write it."[1] None of Leland's writings for the Times could be identified, and no comment on his work could be discovered.

If it can be assumed that "editorial writers" like Hurlbert and Leland occasionally wrote dramatic reviews, then William Swinton's brother John must be included in this list of doubtful critics. He was born on December 12, 1829; after the family migrated to Canada, he became a printer's apprentice, first in Montreal and then in New York, and graduated from the Williston Seminary, Massachusetts in 1853. He returned to printing, then travelled, was active in the Kansas Free-State Movement in 1856, and managed, for a few months, the Lawrence *Republican*. When he returned to New York in 1857, "A casual contribution to the Times brought him to the attention of Henry J. Raymond, who gave him employment." He was on the editorial staff from 1860 to 1870. He resigned, then, to devote his life to the cause of organized labor, writing pamphlets and publishing his own labor journal from 1883 to 1887. From 1875 to 1883, and after 1887, he was chief of the editorial staff of the New York *Sun*. He died on December 15, 1901.[2]

Again, none of his writings for the Times could be identified. The Times itself says that he ". . . was known during his connection with it as one of its most versatile and fluent writers. The department of 'Minor Topics' [on the editorial page] was long under his charge."[3] He himself is reported as saying that he wrote chiefly on medicine, disease and crimes, and that his brother William had told him ". . . how to write for that paper — what subjects to take up — and so I wrote two or three articles which were accepted by Mr. Raymond. This I kept up until Mr. Raymond engaged me as a staff-writer."[4] It is really unlikely that any of his writings, then, included dramatic reviews; the "Minor Topics" column does not contain anything more theatrical than occasional gossip about an actor or a manager. But so long as other editorial writers may have occasionally reviewed plays, John Swinton should at least be men-

1. *Ibid.*; also Pennell, *Charles Godfrey Leland*, II, 246.
2. *Dictionary of American Biography*, XVIII, 252; also Debs, *John Swinton: Radical Editor and Leader, passim.*
3. Jubilee Supplement, 1901, Sept. 18, 11:3 (issued Sept. 25).
4. Waters, *op. cit.*, pp. 12, 28; *passim.*

tioned here.

The remaining three critics are even more obscure, and their connection with the Times even more dubious. All three — James Oakes, Albert E. Lancaster and a man named Fairbanks — are listed by Winter among the notable critics of the period.[1] Oakes seems to be known primarily as the close friend of Edwin Forrest. Montrose Moses assigns him definitely to Boston,[2] but Alger notes that he, having acquired a taste for the theatre early in life, started to write criticisms of plays which he gave to regular reporters for publication, and later contributed his articles under the pseudonym "Acorn" to "several leading journals in the East and South."[3] The Times may, of course, have been included among those, but none of his articles — if there were any — could be identified. Of Lancaster, absolutely nothing is known except that he was the author of "All's Dross But Love" (1889) and the co-author, with Frank Vincent, of "The Lady of Cawnpore" (1891). The Fairbanks mentioned by Winter could either be Charles W. Fairbanks, night editor of the New York *Sun* from 1868,[4] or Charles Bullard Fairbanks (1827-1859), believed to be the author of a book of travel sketches and essays called *My Unknown Chum "Aguecheek,"* and published in 1917 (1912) [*sic*]. Their employment by the Times as drama critics seems highly unlikely; they have been included here merely for the sake of completeness.

Though the biographical outlines are deplorably sketchy, it is possible to reconstruct from them a reasonably clear composite picture of the drama critic of the Times. All those men whose educational background is known seem to have attended college; some, indeed, had extensive graduate training. At least two were teachers themselves. Most seem to have travelled extensively, both before and during their employment as drama critics. Many, also, were creative writers; at least five wrote plays, while others wrote short stories or poetry, adapted plays or, at least, wrote literary articles for newspapers and periodicals. Several must have had a good musical background; there seems to have been no sharp distinction between music and drama criticism, and at least two — Schwab and Seymour — reviewed concerts, opera and ballet along with legitimate plays and semi-musical variety shows, burlesques

1. *The Press and the Stage*, p. 31.
2. *The American Dramatist*, p. 79.
3. *Op. cit.*, II, 625.
4. O'Brien, *The Story of the Sun*, p. 243.

and "spectacles" which naturally fall into the province of drama criticism. Most critics appear also to have had journalistic assignments quite unrelated to drama criticism. O'Brien and Leland wrote articles on art; Seymour, on at least two occasions, worked as special European correspondent; O'Brien, Hurlbert and William Swinton were war correspondents; Schwab was mentioned by the New York *Dramatic News* as "Foreign Night Scissors Editor," and both Hurlbert and Leland were foreign editors.[1]

Financially, the critics seem to have been in a rather precarious position. Of the Bohemian critics, *The Round Table* reports in a vehement attack on the whole group that ". . . When it became desirable that a certain number of lines should be printed each week about theatres, the newspapers took the smart drivel of these Bohemians at penny-a-line rates . . ."[2] The theatrical notices and reviews in the Times averaged about two hundred and thirty lines a week in the sixties, with considerably less in the war years, so that the maximum rate during those two decades, at a penny a line, and when all the notices were written by a single critic, was five dollars a week.[3] It has been impossible to determine when the Times paid its critics regular salaries, and when not; but it seems highly probable that free-lance contributors like O'Brien and Daly were paid by the line, while regularly employed critics received steady salaries. It is also evident that the free-lance critics did not rely on the penny-a-line pay for their dramatic reviews for their entire income; but probably earned considerably more money with their other contributions to newspapers and periodicals. As has already been noted, the New York *Dramatic News* listed Schwab's salary as twenty-five dollars a week in 1875 and thirty-five dollars a week in 1878, and hinted that this salary was so inadequate as to induce him to supplement his income by writing copy for theatrical advertisements and by other, probably less ethical means. Schwab's salary, however, appears to have been far from inadequate by the standard of the 1870s, especially if the high figure is correct. The pay which the free-lance critics received, before the Civil War, was, of course, ridiculously low, and may easily have prompted the

1. Such additional assignments still seem to be the practice today; one needs only recall Brooks Atkinson's wartime articles on Russia.
2. I, 43 (Jan 2, 1864).
3. The figures on the average lineage were arrived at by computing the lineages for each issue during four weeks of each of the following years: 1853, 1855, 1857, 1860, 1866, and 1869.

rumors of the critics' corruption.[1]

It may be of interest to compare the critics' salaries to the Times' income from theatrical advertisements. The agent of the famous primadonna Mme. Sontag, B. Ullman, notes in a letter to the Times in 1853 that the New York *Evening Mirror* charged one hundred and thirty-eight dollars for each notice about Mme. Sontag's concerts, while the other New York newspapers charged between sixty and eighty dollars.[2]   (These notices ran daily from a date about two or three weeks before the engagement started until the day of the last concert.)   In 1877, the Times charged twenty-five cents a line for theatrical advertisements, or, at a daily average of two hundred lines of standard type, three hundred and fifty dollars a week.[3]

Aside from the salary question, the critics met with obstacles that are almost inconceivable today. A press box, or special press section, appears to have been unknown. Some managers distributed free tickets to the critics (frequently under severe protests from other managers and certain publications), but these seem to have been for general admission only; and the integrity and honesty of the managers who distributed these tickets were seriously doubted by a sizeable section of the New York press and theatrical world.[4] The effects of this situation were devastating, and dramatic criticism in the newspapers seems to have survived only because of the sheer tenacity of the press and the amazing resilience of the critics. "Not being able . . . to secure a seat in the ordinary way, and being a stranger to the managerial courtesy of the Chambersstreet [*sic*] Theatre," the critic was unable to attend the opening night of "A Midsummer Night's Dream." However, "Through the intercession of a speculator, we were more fortunate on Saturday . . ."[5] "The

1. The average per capita income for the decade 1874-1883 was $278.- a year, or $5.346 a week (Kuznets, *National Income*, 1946, p. 32). The average weekly salaries of some representative groups of workmen in 1877, for a six-day work-week, follow: Bricklayers (N.Y.) $17.10; Shoemakers (N.J.) $9.06; Bookbinders (N.Y.) $15.48; Proofreaders (Conn.) $18.00; Compositors (N.Y.) $18.06; (Bureau of Labor Statistics, U.S. Department of Labor, *Bulletin No. 604*, "History of Wages in the United States from Colonial Times to 1928," Part II, *passim*).

2. Sept. 8, 4:4.

3. New York *Dramatic News*, III, 1877, Jan. 27, 4:1. The article gives the following rates for other New York newspapers: *Herald*, 40 cents; *Tribune*, 30 cents; *Sun*, 40 cents; *World*, 15 cents. To arrive at the average daily lineage in the Times, fifteen issues were sampled each in January, March, September and December of 1877. The charges for any given advertisement are based on the equivalent number of lines of standard agate type, not on the actual number of printed lines in the advertisement.

4. *The Round Table*, I, 76 (Jan. 16, 1864), and *passim*; New York *Dramatic News*, 1875, Dec. 25, 4:4, and *passim*.

5. Times, 1854, Feb. 6, 1:3.

New York Theatre opened last evening. In consequence of the crowded state of the house and the lack of any kind of provision for the press, we were unable to see or hear a word . . ."[1] At another time, the critic was mangled in the rear of the parquette-circle with hundreds of standees, and thus "Unfortunately, we were unable to hear or judge this drama . . ."[2] Later, however, this situation appears to have improved, for no further complaints by the critics could be discovered.

Unwanted by the theatre owners, hated and maligned by managers, actors and the theatrical journals, frequently caught in the violent battles between rival newspapers, and working under extremely unfavorable conditions, the critics seem to deserve admiration for writing any criticism at all, or perhaps even for merely perpetuating their own kind.

> . . . but there will always be critics. . . . In the theatre, they are the third of an inevitable triumvirate, whose other two members are death and taxes. By now they should feel at home with these somber companions, for the fluctuations of fame never raise them much above death, nor sink them much below taxes. . . . The critics are the whipping boys of an art or the power in restraint of business — whichever is the current view about them. But they will always be on Broadway, make no mistake about that. They will never go away, like bad dreams drifting elsewhere with the dawn.[3]

1. Sept. 19, 4:4.
2. 1856, Nov. 18, 4:5.
3. Nichols, *op. cit.*, 17:1.

II

THE REVIEWS

The Times began publication on September 18, 1851, as an eight-page newspaper of tabloid size, appearing daily except Sundays. Each page consisted of six columns; approximately two pages of each issue were devoted to advertisements and special and commercial notices. With few exceptions, the first and eighth pages were devoted to news exclusively, the second to news and feature articles, book reviews and the like, the fourth to editorials, and the remainder was split between news and advertising. During the first year of publication some evening editions were issued. In 1861, the first Sunday edition appeared, and in 1867 the format was changed to a seven-column page. From that year on, also, at least two issues weekly consisted of either twelve-page "triple-sheets" or the usual eight pages with a four-page supplement. In those, usually one additional page was devoted to advertising, two to news, and one to features, and the editorials appeared on page six. There were no illustrations, except for occasional maps and graphs, and except for the Union Army's eagle which adorned the headlines on Victory Day in 1865.

Prior to the first issue, the co-founder and co-publisher of the Times, Henry Jarvis Raymond, published a prospectus which stated, as one of the aims and intentions of the publishers, that *"The Times* will present daily: . . . Criticisms of music, the drama, painting, and of whatever in any department of art may merit . . . attention."[1] A statement in the first issue was somewhat more explicit: "As for amusements, we shall bring them in our range very much as inclination may prompt, and shall render them over in epitome, or in critique, to those who have a liking for our offhand opinions."[2] Less than one and a half years later, the Times emphatically renounced this rather lackadaisical policy:

1. Quoted in Maverick, *Henry J. Raymond and the New York Press for Thirty Years,* p. 93, and reprinted in the Times, 1851, Sept. 24, 4:6.
2. Sept. 18, 2:4.

> . . . Just now, there seems to be more need of a wholesome critical cen-
> sorship than ever. . . . The system of theatrical notice adopted hitherto
> by the principal papers . . . is a mere farce. Notices . . . are constructed
> mechanically — written without knowledge, and critical without judg-
> ment. They are mere advertisements. . . . It is our intention to devote
> more space than we have hitherto done, to theatrical and musical crit-
> icism. . . . Our present remarks are merely preparatory to entering fully
> and frequently on such subjects, and submitting to the public careful,
> candid and impartial criticisms.[1]

In the early issues, theatrical notices really were "mere advertisements." They usually ran under a heading "New York City" along
with fires, accidents, suicides and crimes, sometimes under the subheading "Amusements This Evening," and gave rarely more than
the theatre, the name of the piece to be performed, and the outstanding members of the cast. Such listings appeared almost every
day, In addition to them, the Times published some items of theatrical news, with the stress on news rather than on theatrical; in
the first issue, such an item noted the arrival of "Miss Addison,
well spoken of as an actress, and the return of that successful comedian Mr. Hackett."[2]   On September 24, the amusements list included mention of "The first concert of Miss Catherine Hayes . . .
at Tripler Hall . . ."; the writer candidly states that "At this time
we shall not attempt a criticism . . ." and proceeded merely to de-
describe the concert hall and the audience.[3]

Throughout the first year of publication, musical items predominate in these lists, and the few theatrical notices cannot be called
critical by any stretch of the imagination.   Only very few even
venture such remarks as that a play "continues a successful run,"
and all extended critical analyses are confined to musical matters.
The first theatrical item that, in my opinion, contains enough
critical analysis to be called a review appeared on September 11,
1852, almost a full year after the Times had begun publication; it
is about thirty lines long and, as a "first," is probably worth quoting in full:

> — The Bateman children made their first appearance since their re-
> turn from Europe on Thursday evening. They were well received, but
> such tragedies as Richard III, are not calculated to display their talents
> to the best advantage. The most correct reading by two young children
> cannot dispel the feeling that the performance is a burlesque. They
> should have plays written for them, as in suitable characters they are

Editorial, 1853, Jan. 17, 4:3.
2. 1851, Sept. 18, 4:2.
3. 2:5.

unsurpassed. In the farce of the 'Young Couple,' they appear to better advantage, for their youth and size harmonize with the plot. Their acting here was surprising, and the audience seemed much better pleased than with their attempt at tragedy. At the close of the farce, they were 'called out,' and made the target for a broadside of bouquets. They gracefully acknowledged these compliments, and 'Charley' made a brief address. The audience was not so large as should have greeted the children, but when they become better known they cannot fail to have full houses.[1]

From then on, theatrical notices appeared more and more frequently, gradually grew longer and more detailed, and contained more and more criticism. In the lists of amusements, each establishment had a notice of one paragraph consisting of anywhere from three to fifteen lines. The lists appeared, in October of 1852, in seventeen of a total of twenty-six issues (there were five Sundays that October); of these seventeen, thirteen appeared on the front-page, two on the editorial page (page four), one on page five and one – in the then rare editions containing supplements – on page nine. Most of them were musical, and most of them were still quasi-advertisements; but critical remarks, such as that Forrest seems to be better in "Jack Cade" than in "Hamlet," were no longer rare.

By 1853, the dramatic review was firmly established, possibly as the result of the new policy adopted in January of that year. The notices had definitely deserted the column listing news of the city, and had established a column in their own right, headed variously "Amusements" and "Dramatic and Musical." In March of this year, one review ran almost four-fifths of a column in length,[2] five others ran from three to eight paragraphs each, and shorter notices appeared on eleven days, besides.

In the following year, the theatrical columns moved off the frontpage and onto page four, where they were usually printed immediately after the editorials. That became their permanent place for the entire period under study, with few exceptions; only in the mid-fifties could a review still be found on the frontpage, and later an abundance of editorial matter, or news running over onto the editorial page, would occasionally push the theatre column onto the page following the editorials.

In 1854, too, reviews became limited to certain days of the week. Saturdays and Mondays were usually devoted to weekly previews and summaries, with the actual notices and critiques of plays ap-

1. 2:4.
2. "The White Slave of England," at the Broadway Theatre, March 1, 4:4.

pearing, on the average, three days a week, ordinarily on Tuesdays, Wednesdays, and Thursdays. Musical reviews still predominated in these columns, in this and the next few years; in March of 1855, for example, the Times ran seventeen musical notices and reviews, but only nine theatrical items.

By 1857, the physical set-up of the amusement columns had become fairly regular. On Mondays, there would be a weekly preview; and in this as well as in the daily theatrical columns each notice or critique would appear under the name of the theatre used as a subheading. Throughout, of course, the reviewer used the editorial "we." In 1860, the Monday previews were replaced with Saturday summaries of events; otherwise the procedure remained unchanged.

Prior to the Civil War, the theatrical columns had to give way occasionally to political news, when such news, for some reason, became unusually heavy. Thus little more than brief summaries of theatrical events were published during the months of 1852 and 1853 when Webster's death occupied as much as sixty percent of all space not reserved for advertising matter; in the following year, the Crimean War dominated the news to such an extent that there was little room for amusements; every year, when the Congressional and State legislative sessions started, the space available for theatrical notices was cut; and little theatrical news was published during Presidential campaigns and elections. Occasionally, some spectacular occurrence in the amusement field would force the omission of routine notices and reviews; thus, when the Times ran a full-column article on the closing of the Academy of Music, in 1855, the following notice appeared:

> CROWDED OUT. — Notices of Miss Makeah's appearance at the Broadway, and of a new piece called 'Aggravating Sam' at Burton's.[1]

These notices were then printed on the following day.

During the Civil War, the war news frequently "crowded out" the news and reviews of theatrical events, although a general listing and summary still appeared at least once a week; and the same was true during the months immediately following the end of the war and Lincoln's assassination. But in 1867 the reviews — by now full-length articles giving a complete summary for the theatre-going public — appeared almost daily; in October of that year, every single premiere of importance was reviewed. The physical make-

1. March 6, 4:4.

up, however, did not change; all the reviews and notices of one day still occupied one to one and a half columns, with separate sub-headings for each theatre whose offering was noted. In 1868, a special section called "Dramatic Notes" was added to the Sunday column summarizing the events of the past and coming weeks; this section was devoted to theatrical news from cities other than New York, with a special sub-section reserved for foreign news, primarily from London and Paris. In 1869 and 1870, these Sunday articles contained various sections in addition to the main summary of events in New York: "Yesterday's Incidents," "Home Notes" and the like were used for gossipy items, usually of one sentence each, about the American stage; while "The Foreign Stage" formed a separate section, with its own sub-headings such as "New Drama in London" or "The French Drama," But the daily amusement column remained essentially unchanged from its 1867 form. By 1870, however, the Sunday articles had increased in overall length to two, sometimes even two and a-half columns, or, roughly, four percent of the total space not devoted to advertisements. In the daily newspaper, the amusement column occupied about two percent of the non-advertising space.[1]

There was little change in the physical make-up of the amusement column between 1870 and 1880. In 1875, the Sunday column was divided into musical and dramatic sections — the first time that such a classification was sustained for a number of weeks. The daily columns still frequently ran notices of concerts, operas, and legitimate plays side by side, even though occasionally a division had been attempted. The number of twelve-page editions had vastly increased by the time — there were about four a week — but the amusement column still followed the editorials, either on the same or on the following page. From 1875 on, summaries of the week's events appeared frequently on Saturdays as well as on Sundays, although the Saturday columns were usually much shorter, and rarely carried news of the stage outside of New York City.

It was pointed out earlier that the Times occasionally suppressed the amusement column, or at least a major portion of it, because of an overabundance of more important news. However, I doubt that the Times' failure to review theatrical offerings can always,

1. These estimates are based on an actual count of news columnage for one week each in March and April of 1870. The percentages are rather amazing in view of the fact that in this year the reconstruction of the South was still of vast news interest, and that for the Times, in addition, this was the climactic year before the exposure of the Tweed Ring.

without exception be ascribed to a heavy news volume. It appears that offerings which were just on the fringe of "legitimate theatre" — variety shows, burlesques, minstrel and aquatic shows, equestrian, canine or other animal performances, and some of the indefinable offerings in Barnum's Museum — were rarely reviewed in the Times, probably because the publishers, or the critics, did not want to dignify them by devoting to them the attention and space usually accorded to Wallack's, Burton's, Daly's and the other playhouses. It seems safe to say that the Times reviewed such performances only when they were outstandingly vulgar or outstandingly bad, or when, shocking the whole theatrical world, an actor of note appeared in them.

In addition, it must be remembered that most of the legitimate New York theatres of this period offered a new play at least once in three weeks, sometimes as many as three in one week, and even more in such engagements as Forrest's which were on a repertory basis. Obviously, the Times' critic — especially when he wrote both the musical and the dramatic reviews — could not possibly cover all noteworthy events in a week topheavy with premieres, and so some events inevitably went unnoticed.

Another possible reason for these omissions is cited by *The Round Table*, an avowed enemy of the newspapers' dramatic departments, and could not be substantiated elsewhere. This journal suggests that "several" of the New York newspapers refused to review offerings by managers who did not use the newspapers' print-shop for their playbills, and that they also required a minimum of advertising by a given theatre before reviewing its productions.[1] If these charges are true, then, evidently, the newspapers did not review the performances of a company whose manager was not sufficiently tractable.

The Times itself was apparently guilty of one grave omission for a reason completely different from those given above — an omission all the more grave because it concerned one of the outstanding actors of the period, Edwin Forrest. Forrest became involved in his unsavory divorce suit at just about the same time that the Times began publication, and the Times — along with most of the New York press — sided against him. From December 22, 1851, until the divorce was granted, the Times devoted to the trial an average of one and a half columns each day on which the court was in ses-

---

1. "The Theatres and the Newspapers," I, 59-60 (Jan. 9, 1864).

sion, giving the full text of the proceedings. The day after the
trial ended — January 26, 1852 — a perfectly vicious editorial condemned Forrest bitterly, and added that "He may possibly con-
tinue to crowd the galleries of our second-rate theatres, and to receive the applause of the reckless mob."[1] Undoubtedly because
of this antagonism to Forrest, the Times rarely reviewed any of his
performances, and in the few reviews that it did accord him, he was
criticized mercilessly. His engagement at the Broadway Theatre in
February and March, 1852, was merely noted in the amusement
lists; not a single performance was reviewed. The end of this engagement, in April, also went unnoticed. His opening in Bulwer's
"Richelieu," in the following season, was briefly noted; his rather
melodramatic way of acting was violently denounced, and there
was, in the notice, a rather sarcastic reference to the divorce case —
proof enough, I believe, that the Times, or at least its reviewer, was
deeply prejudiced against Forrest because of the unfortunate scandal.[2] During this season, Forrest's performances were reviewed
only once more; in this article two paragraphs were devoted to a
denunciation of Forrest's acting in "Jack Cade," while over a column was used to discuss the historical background of the play.[3]

Forrest died in 1872, and for those twenty years I found only
four more reviews of his performances; all were equally brief and
unfavorable.[4] The fact that his repertory was seldom varied, and
that he himself was admittedly on the decline, is hardly an adequate explanation of this situation, especially since he was still extremely popular, and commanded a sizeable audience during his
annual engagements. The conclusion that the Times ignored him
out of prejudice appears thus inescapable.

Despite all these omissions, it is safe to say that the majority of
the plays which opened during the period under study were reviewed in the Times. And these reviews not only grew in length
and frequency, but developed, perhaps even more rapidly, from
minor, uncritical notices to analytical articles covering every essen-
tial phase of a given theatrical performance.

The first critical notice — that of the Bateman children — was
singularly uninformative; it mentioned neither the authors of the

1. 2:1.
2. 1852, Sept. 21, 1:1. The reviewer was probably either O'Brien or Seymour.
3. Oct. 20, 2:5.
4. 1853, Feb. 4, 3:3; May 4, 1:2; 1855, Apr. 24, 4:5; 1867, Sept. 3, 5:1. It must be
remembered, however, that only two months for each year from 1857 to 1879 were
used in this research.

plays, nor the place of the performance, nor the names of the manager and other members of the cast (if any). It only noted briefly
the Bateman children's acting and the reaction of the audience.
In contrast, a musical notice of the same month, even though only
three paragraphs long, was considerably closer to what we would
call a full-scale review: It gave Mme. Alboni's entire program for the
concert, listed her assistants, and gave some analysis of her rendition of the individual numbers.[1] In the theatrical notices, during
November of 1852, most of the stress is placed on the acting of the
star; the theatre is usually mentioned only in the headings, and the
author is usually ignored. Whatever critical analysis these notices
contain is directed at the performance rather than at the play itself.[2]   In December, a thirty-nine-line notice of Mrs. Mowatt's
"Armand" criticizes not only her performance, but also points out
certain similarities between her play and Bulwer's "Lady of Lyons;"
and the same theme is pursued on the following day in a review of
her performance in Talfourd's "Ion."[3] This theme of plagiarism,
or "adaptation," as the kindly critics often called it, occupies an
unusual amount of space in the reviews throughout this period.
though the critics made careful distinctions between a playwright's
repetitious use of his own materials, outright plagiarism, transla-
tions and adaptations of foreign (usually French) plays, and drama-
tizations of proseworks. Hardly a week goes by during the theatrical seasons of any of these thirty-odd years during which some
such production is not discussed at length, frequently with a good
deal of derision and sometimes with a sincere despondency over
the lack of originality among the contemporary playwrights. Thus
the first theatrical review of 1853, seventy-five lines long, is devoted
in its entirety to Burton's dramatization of *Nicholas Nickleby*; all
other aspects of the performance are either ignored or mentioned
only in passing.[4]
    Rapidly, however, the critics extended their notices to other as-
pects of the stage. A two-paragraph notice of the younger Colman's

    1. 1852, Sept. 15, 2:3.
    2. On November 11 (2:6), E. G. Holland's tragedy "The Highland Treason" was re-
viewed upon publication, not as a performance but as a book; and this review was very
complete indeed: It summarized the plot, criticized its violation of the unities and its
occasional ludicrous effects, and gave quotations to substantiate the writer's opinions.
It was not until considerably later that such a detailed analysis was applied to stage performances.
    3. Dec. 3, 1:1; Dec. 4, 1:4.
    4. Jan. 21, 4:6. Similarly, a two-third column review (Oct. 14, 4:3) of Brougham's
adaptation of *Bleak House* was devoted almost entirely to a comparison of the play and
the novel.

"Heir-at-Law," performed at Wallack's,[1] gives a cursory glance over Old English comedies as a whole, thus foreshadowing the inclusion of "background" material in the longer critical articles of later decades. Three weeks later a four-paragraph notice for the first time gives a brief summary of a play's plot.[2] Gradually, thereafter, the plot summaries became standard practice for reviews of all but the best-known plays, even though the critics appeared at times at a loss to understand — let alone to explain to others — the intricacies of the action in some of the plays written during the period.

There were other drastic developments in the art of criticism in the Times during this year of 1853 — all probably due to the promise of greater attention to theatrical matters made in the January editorial which was quoted earlier. The criticism of individual actors' performances took on a new note, the first inkling (in the Times, at least) of the growing revolt, upon the stage and in the audience, against the conventional, hyper-stylized way of acting. This is only vaguely implicit in a review of Forrest as Macbeth: "He is alternately nasal and bronchial in a most unpleasant way. When he is not whispering, he is muttering . . . [or] attempting new readings in violation of taste and ordinary delicacy."[3] Only a week later, a review of "The Merchant of Venice" at Wallack's[4] violently denounces the actors' traditional stress on "points," indicating much more definitely than in the Forrest review the trend toward more realistic acting. On the following day similar criticism is made of the acting in "Much Ado About Nothing," at the same theatre; and a new element is added to the Times' dramatic reviews with a rather detailed description of the scenery.[5] Also, during the same month, a review of the performances at the Hippodrome concentrates for the first time on the ethic-aesthetic basis of theatrical performances as a whole, criticizing the circus plays as below the dignity of an audience which lays some claims to culture and cosmopolitanism.[6] This review was followed by an editorial and by a feature article on the same theme[7] — a theme which was pursued by the Times throughout the period under

1. March 1, 4:4.
2. "To Paris and Back for Five Pounds," March 21, 1:2.
3. May 4, 1:2
4. May 11, 4:4.
5. May 12, 1:6.
6. May 5, 1:3.
7. May 16, 4:2; May 27, 2:3.

study. The Times, apparently much like the clergy during those years, was opposed to the theatre as an essentially immoral institution; it was willing to praise it whenever it contributed to the intellectual life of the city, but ready to detect and excoriate the slightest trace of levity, superficiality or immorality.[1]

The reviews of that month conclude the first season of active dramatic criticism in the Times, and by this time certain elements of theatrical performances — the acting, the plot, the background and sources of the play, its moral effects and, at least once, the scenery — have not only been introduced, but have evidently become more or less permanent parts of the reviews. Some of them still appear only rarely, to be sure; and much of what is said about these elements is undoubtedly immature and sometimes even primitive. But it seems to me that the impression of an ever-growing awareness of the manifold aspects of the theatre is inescapable, whether this impression is to be attributed to the individual critics or to the newspaper as a whole.

During the following season, some new elements were added. The trend toward realism, so far directed toward the acting, is extended to the plot in a review of Fletcher's "The Elder Brother," revived at the Broadway. Fletcher's plays were considered so unrealistic that only good characterization saved them from oblivion. This same review, also for the first time, touches on the production as a whole, criticizing the manager for presenting a play that was evidently ill rehearsed and staged much too hastily.[2] Two successive reviews of two plays by Boucicault — "Love and Money," at Wallack's, and "The Fox Hunt," at Burton's — attend for the first time to characterization and dialogue.[3] A review, three quarters of a column long, of Brougham's "Game of Life" is devoted almost in its entirety to the fact that the play was apparently written to be acted by Wallack's company, and for no other purpose;[4] and thus, for the first time, the critic mentions this "vehicle" type of play, and stresses the peculiar talents of individual companies. The reviews now almost invariably identify the more important members of the cast, usually not in a special tabulation (which, I believe, did not become common usage until the Twentieth Century), but in the discussion of either the acting or the plot. The

1. Further examples of this trend will be cited in their approximate chronological order.
2. Nov. 2, 4:4.
3. Nov. 8, 4:4; Nov. 24, 4:4.
4. Dec. 13, 4:4.

controversy over repertory theatres is mentioned for the first time, and poor Forrest is again the victim of a brief article vigorously attacking the lack of variety in his selections.[1] Toward the end of the season, a review of "The Tempest," at Burton's, criticizes the company's interpretation of the text, and adds still another phase of theatre life to the scope of the reviews: Make-up.[2] Finally, for this season, a review of "The Merchant of Venice" for the first time refers to an earlier production of the same play by the same company.[3]

By the time that the next season (1854-1855) opened, the general content of the reviews was as firmly established as their physical lay-out. Naturally, not every review included all the various aspects of the performance, though most of them referred to the plot and the acting; the other elements, however, were mentioned only as they impressed the critics in any given performance. And, as the occasion arose, still new elements were included: A review of the first presentation in a new theatre would go into a detailed description of the size and furnishings of the house,[4] or, prior to the debut of a star from out-of-town, as in the case of Miss Makeah,[5] the critic would discuss the star's earlier career, and describe the schedule of her engagement in New York. In the case of benefit performances, a critical review would usually be replaced by a brief description of their purpose and their reception by the public.[6] A review of Victor Hugo's "Lucrezia Borgia," at the New York Theater, concentrated to some extent on the poetic techniques of the adaptation.[7] Some unjustified criticism of Burton's "A Nice Young Man," dealing with a French play on which Burton's comedy was allegedly modeled, was promptly retracted on the following day.[8] The tabular form for listing the cast of a performance was used for the first time in a review of Mrs. Centlivre's "Busy Body," at Wallack's; as indicated before, this form was used only rarely in the period under study. Otherwise, this review is sufficiently typical of the level of dramatic criticism reached in the Times by this time that some excerpts of it are rather revealing, es-

1. 1854, Apr. 10, 4:5.
2. Apr. 12, 4:5.
3. May 18, 4:5.
4. For example, the review of "The Wife" at the New York (Metropolitan) Theatre, 1854, Sept. 21, 4:4.
5. Sept. 27, 4:4.
6. For example, Oct. 2, 4:3.
7. Oct. 6, 4:4.
8. Dec. 27, 4:5; Dec. 28, 4:5.

pecially when compared with the review of the Bateman children's
performance printed some two and a half years earlier:

WALLACK'S THEATRE. — For a change, there are few things more
acceptable than an old English Comedy. It is historically interesting to
descend into that giddy Maelstrom of twaddle and intrigue — a seven-
teenth century plot. The journey may be accomplished with a few moral
bumps, and our conventional ideas as to virtue, matrimony and similar
absurdities may be slightly deranged thereby. But when we float to the
surface again, we can generally afford to laugh at the adventure, for it
don't [*sic*] happen — and we don't want it to happen — every day.
Some Comedies there are that bear revival satisfactory [*sic*]; others
that never should be revived; things that are carrion in the country that
gave them birth, and which, as age progresses, must exhale a more
hideous odor even than now. Still there is an ample catalogue whence
selection can be made, and Mr. Wallack has resorted to it judiciously, in
selecting Mrs. Centlivre's comedy of the 'Busy Body.' This work has not
been seen on the stage for some years; is unobjectionable in every
sense, and affords ample opportunity for good, sprightly acting, pretty
costumes, scenery, *et cetera*.

The moral of the story on which this amusing comedy is constructed
teaches that neither parents nor guardians should force the inclinations
(matrimonial, or course) of the young ladies under their charge; and
inversely that 'bolts and bars fly asunder' when youth and love whisper
the needful 'open Sesame.' In addition to this domestic lesson, we gain
an instructive morsel of worldly wisdom from the career of *Marplot* —
the busy body — who from the eccentric habit of putting his nose into
every one's business, very often gets it pulled; and although one of the
best fellows in the world, receives as a punishment for his inveterate
curiosity more canings than a modern dramatist would care to put on
an actor's back. . . .

So far, it should be noted, the review is considerably more mature
than those of two or three years before; its style, though perhaps a
little facetious, makes easy and pleasant reading, and the plot is
sketched in brief terms rather than given in an act-by-act outline.
At the same time, the stress on morality, on the instructive aspects
of the theatre, is perfectly obvious; the critic evidently guides himself by Johnson's dictum that "the end of poetry is to instruct by
pleasing."

The review continues with a tabular listing of the cast, and with
a discussion of the performance by individual actors; for example:

Mrs. Hoey played the character [of Miranda] in an easy lady like way;
and looked charming and coaxing enough for an older man than
Gripe. . . .

Come we now to *Sir Francis Gripe*. All the incidents in the play indicate the character of this man as hard, cruel, avaricious and villainous. For four acts and a half Mr. Blake delineates a totally different character, he is mild unctuous, contented . . . His conduct in turning around finally and cursing everybody is inexplicable. . . . . The fault of Mr. Blake's interpretation is that he makes *Sir Francis* a great deal too agreeable. . . .

And the review concludes:

Mr. Wallack has placed this comedy on the stage in his best manner. The costumes are rich, elegant and correct. Some excellent scenery has also been painted . . . and altogether we can recommend the entertainment as an enjoyable way to spend an evening.[1]

The considerably higher level of critical achievement at this time, in comparison to the reviews which appeared only two or three years previously, is also evident in a review, about one-third of a column long, of Shakespeare's "Coriolanus" at the Broadway, with Edwin Forrest. Forrest, of course, received his usual "panning," and the production as a whole was heartily criticized. The critic, however, gave a careful and intelligent analysis of the play on the basis of the text, and showed irrefutably how Forrest and some other members of the cast had misunderstood, and therefore misrepresented, the characters of the play. Forrest, for example, was said to have interpreted Coriolanus as weak and even sentimental in the scenes with his mother, and in the final scenes with Aufidius.[2]

In the reviews of this period there is also evidence that the critics had a fine understanding for the limitations of the theatre as a medium for information and entertainment, and it seems likely that their criticisms on this basis reflect the reaction of the entire audience. Thus, Burton's adaptation of Dumas' "The Youthful Days of Louis XIV" was criticized for its intolerable length (four and a-half hours on opening night) and for too large a cast of characters; the critic held both of these factors responsible for destroying the unity, and therewith the entire effect, of the presentation.[3] On the occasion of E. L. Davenport's performance of "Love and Loyalty," at the Broadway, the critic took the audience to task for virtually forcing the popular actor to make a speech, not only at the beginning or the end of the play, but even at the end of indi-

[1]. 1855, Feb. 27, 4:3.
[2]. 1855, Apr. 24, 4:5.
[3]. May 8, 4:3.

vidual scenes and acts, when certain "points" had been particularly
well taken. With a sensitivity rarely attributed to the allegedly
hard-boiled critics, the Times' reviewer chided the audience for
thus destroying the dramatic illusion, the very essence of the theatre.[1]

The next season opened with one of the greatest sensations of
the century — the tour of Mlle. Rachel. The handling of her engagement by the Times is well worth detailed study, since, in my
opinion, it represents dramatic criticism of the daily newspapers
at its finest and most useful; while it reflects at the same time certain factors, completely outside the realm of aesthetic criticism,
which nevertheless influenced the style and form of the reviews.

For the beginning of the engagement, the Times apparently allot-
ted an unusual amount of space, and it wisely assigned to the task
of reviewing these performances a man who combined complete
mastery of French, a thorough academic knowledge of French
classical literature, a keen understanding and appreciation of the
theatre, and a shrewd perception of the limitations of the theatre
audience as well as of the Times' readers: William Swinton. Swinton began his series of reviews on the eve of Rachel's first performance with a masterly article, over one and a quarter columns long,
which included a preview of the engagement, a summary of Rachel's
career, and a scholarly discussion of French tragedy in general, and
some advance remarks on the first performance, Corneille's "Les
Horaces." He tried immediately at the outset to direct the attention of his readers to the uniqueness of the event: "Tomorrow every
one will say it marks an epoch in the history of American art. Not
only is this remarkable *tragedienne* the greatest artist of her age, but
the sole representative of a drama which would otherwise be dead
..." This last clause afforded him an easy transition to the subject of French tragedy. "We are all tolerably familiar with the modern French drama, for in truth is it not our own? Do we not crib
it with eagerness ...? But French tragedy is an article which no
country has had the hardihood to steal." With this gentle satire,
it seems to me, he would inevitably have captured the interest of
those of his readers who are familiar with, and have probably tired
of, the plays of Planche and his American and British imitators.
Swinton proceeded to discuss the formality of French tragedy, to
compare it with Elizabethan drama and with its classic ancestors,
to cite in detail the Aristotelian "rules" and to describe the kind of

1. May 16, 4:4.

play that their strict interpretation and application would produce. Next, he discussed, in familiar terms, the versification, and ended his article with a brief but concise resume of the plot of "Les Horaces." He ignored the difficulties that the audience would probably have with the language, partly to avoid frightening them away, and partly to flatter them by implying that this would not be an obstacle to their enjoyment of the play. Throughout the article, Swinton never assumed the tone of a schoolmaster toward his pupils, nor that of the initiated toward the laity.[1]

The review of Rachel's performance, on the following day, occupied about four-fifths of a column. It began with a description of the size of the audience, then briefly noted the confusion which arose over the curtain raiser "Les Droits de l'Homme" (which most of the audience thought to be the first act of Corneille's play), and added some remarks on its plot; then Swinton gave the cast for the tragedy, noted the omission of the fifth act which was "...condemned by the universal voice of French criticism, as a deviation from the writers of the classic stage," and ended with a eulogizing description of Rachel's acting and a note on her reception by the audience.[2] On the following day, the Times printed another article on Rachel's opening night, a very satirical piece which ridiculed the audience for the confusion over the curtain-raiser and the obvious language difficulties, and which chose as its special target those among the audience who only attended for the sake of being able to say that they had seen Rachel.[3]

In the adjoining column, Swinton, reviewing Rachel's second rendition, also dealt a blow at that part of the audience, by noting sarcastically the rapid decline in attendance; but the by far greater part of his review is devoted to the plot of Racine's "Phedre," its verse, a comparison between Racine and Corneille, and another detailed analysis of Rachel's acting. The third review, of "Adrienne Lecouvreur," followed the same basic structure: It first described briefly the audience, and then treated, in this order, the plot, the background of the play, the cast, and Rachel's acting.[4] This sequence was used for every subsequent review of her performances, except when certain plays were repeated, and in those cases the reviews

1. Sept. 3, 4:4.
2. Sept. 4, 4:4.
3. Sept. 5, 4:4. This article may not be by Swinton, since its style is totally different from the others definitely identified as his.
4. Sept. 7, 4:5.

treated only the differences, if any, between the first and the repeat performances.   The reviews, however, decreased in length,
mainly because Swinton no longer needed to give as much background material as he did for the first few performances; from the
third review on, they varied from one-third to two-thirds of a column in length.

The first Monday review after Rachel's opening night not only
briefly summarized her performances to that date, but also quoted
extensively from the reviews in the other New York newspapers.[1]
The following Saturday review again summarized her performances
to date.[2]

In the meantime, the Times had editorially joined the other New
York newspapers in condemning the unusually high prices charged
by the Academy of Music for tickets for the Rachel performances,
and Swinton's reviews, in the parts dealing with the audience, occasionally referred to this issue. He tried as best he could to review
the presentations without bias, but especially toward the end of the
New York engagement, his criticism reflects the fact that the engagement had failed because of purely external matters — the prices
and the language. He could not avoid stating at least implicitly what
the editorial writers stated bluntly and acidly: that Rachel's manager had failed to recognize that in New York the theatre belonged
to the public as a whole rather than to a small intellectual elite,
and that therefore the success of the entire venture was doomed
from the start.   The issue ended climactically on November 6,
when the leading article in the Times was a report by its Paris correspondent Dick Tinto on the devastating attack on the New York
audience by the Parisian critics, especially Jules Janin; the article
ended with Tinto's refutation of their criticism, which was further
elaborated in an editorial on the same day.[3]

The Rachel engagement was a milestone in criticism in the Times
as well as in New York's theatrical history; there were, however,
some other, though minor, developments in dramatic criticism during this season which are worth mentioning. Boker's "Francesca da
Rimini" had its premiere at the Broadway; the review praised not
only the play itself and the acting, but also the careful staging, giving special praise to the costumes.[4]   Four weeks later, Burton's

1. Sept. 10, 4:4.
2. Sept. 15, 4:3.
3. Nov. 6, 1:1; Nov. 6, 4:3.
4. Sept. 28, 4:4.

and Wallack's presented the same play on the same night — "The Man of Many Friends" — and the review, though brief, included some caustic comment on the rivalry between the two companies.[1] On the whole, the reviews have by this time attained a higher literary level, particularly through the use of the kind of satire in unfavorable criticism which Seymour used in his article on the London stage. Thus a production of William Bennett's "Love and Revenge," at the New York Theatre, was denounced for "unwilling scenery, unready artists, unnatural situations and unending deaths."[2] Similarly, a three-paragraph review of "Rule a Wife and Have a Wife," at Wallack's, says, much in the style used now by Wolcott Gibbs, that the only things worth seeing in this presentation are the fabulous comb used by Mrs. Hoey as part of her costume, and "Mr. Brougham's unmentionables."[3]

Occasionally, however, the reviews voiced what must seem to us rather strange opinions, indicating perhaps that criticism in the Times had not yet reached full maturity. Thus the critic, in a two-paragraph notice of an amateur performance of "Hamlet" at the Academy of Music, says that "Amateur performances must be very bad to be interesting to the public through the columns of a newspaper. As this was not the case . . . we do not propose entering into detailed criticism."[4] This recalls to mind an earlier performance of "Hamlet" — James Anderson's at the Broadway — in which the critic was obviously unable to cope with his subject, and virtually admitted it:

> It is almost impossible to write a criticism of any actor's performance of a character like *Hamlet* unless, indeed, it is a very bad one. The salient points of that wonderful creation have been so ably expounded by cotemporary [sic] criticism, that it is almost impossible for an intelligent man to mistake them.

That was all the critic was able to say about Anderson's acting in this review,[5] a review which contrasts sadly with some of the really brilliant analyses of Shakespearean performances during the late seventies.

The season of 1855-1856 also saw the first review of a burlesque, the Marsh Troupe's presentation of "Beauty and the Beast," which

1. Oct. 25, 4:4. Further comment on this theme appeared Nov. 3, 4:3.
2. Nov. 17, 4:5.
3. Nov. 27, 4:4.
4. Nov. 28, 4:4.
5. 1853, Oct. 25, 1:3.

was praised for its divergence from the ordinary stage fare.[1] Two days later, a review of "A California Widow," at Wallack's, condemns the use of strong language, and cites "hell" and "damn" as examples — a return to the theme of stage immorality.[2] This theme was further pursued in a very ironic article on the opening of Laura Keene's Variety Theatre — a theatre which was to devote itself chiefly to melodramas, revues and farces of undoubted sex appeal but questionable artistic merit.[3] And again, this season, a review is devoted in part to the purely external factors in stage performances; the critic scores the Broadway Theatre's management for permitting too much distracting noise behind the scenes during a performance of "Herne, the Hunter," and for destroying the effect of the piece by making the intermission too long.[4]

In addition to the "morality" theme, which is pursued by the critics throughout this period, there is another which recurs continuously both in the reviews and in the editorials and special articles: the growth of a National American Drama. Some inkling of this theme is already given in the discussion of the audience of Rachel's performances, where its peculiar democratic character is stressed; the theme is implied in virtually every review in which "adaptations" from the French are discussed, and it is finally brought to the fore in a review of Wilkins' "My Wife's Mirror," produced at the Variety Theatre, which lauds the play as one of the early steps in the direction of original, native American comedy.[5] Later reviews and articles on this subject actually do not offer any definite program by which a national drama can be achieved, nor do they even define the term; but they do reflect a general trend toward artistic independence.

And the movement toward stage realism continues. A play, "Vice and Virtue," at Burton's, was bitterly criticized for a poor plot and poorer acting; at the end of the review the critic says: "The play progressed heavily, but terminated with . . . a mad scene, in which Mrs. Barrow goes through all the usual business pertaining to stage insanity, and draws tears from the tender-hearted."[6] During the same season (1856-1857), an excellent example of the Times' opposition to "immoral" plays occurred. Matilda Heron was

1. 1855, Dec. 11, 4:3.
2. Dec. 13, 4:4.
3. Dec. 28, 4:5.
4. 1856, Feb. 19, 4:5.
5. May 13, 4:3.
6. 1857, Jan. 21, 4:5.

admittedly successful in her performance of "Medea," at Wallack's, and her characterization was widely acclaimed, but the Times' critic thought the play too gory, Medea's murder of her children too unnatural, too distant from Nineteenth Century morals, so that ". . . the play as a play can never be popular . . ."[1]

Also during this season, for the first time, a review in the Times discussed the biographical background of a playwright, on the opening of Mrs. Howe's "The World's Own," at Wallack's.[2] And the season ends with another sensational occurrence: Edwin Booth's debut in New York. The Times devoted thirty-five lines to it, and all but two were a eulogy on his performance as Richard III.[3]

Immediately at the beginning of the next season, a situation similar to "Medea" arose, and again Miss Heron was the unfortunate victim. This time, she starred in a play called "Fiammina," translated from the French and produced at Wallack's; the critic briefly summarized the plot, in which a "bad" woman does not get her just deserts, deplores the effect that such a play would have on the young members of the audience and concludes that "There is no pleasure in praising the acting of Miss Heron under circumstances so depressing as these"[4] The "old" drama came in for its share of criticism again, when Thomas Morton's adaptation of the German "Judith of Geneva" was scored as "a romantic drama of the atrocious school";[5] evidently the New York critics had their fill of Kotzebue and his imitators. When the Broadway Theatre reopened for the season, the review of its first production noted the management's financial status – a rather unusual item for dramatic critiques.[6] (Later on, such matters were usually confined to the column of theatrical news and notes in the week-end issues.) Later during that season, Ronzani's Ballet opened at this theatre, and the first review of its renditions included a definition of the ballet, and a description of all the various elements of which it consists.[7] A review of the farce "My Son Diana," at Laura Keene's, again took up the theme of the American Comedy, this time chiding playwrights for considering nothing a comedy unless it consisted of three long acts, and exhorting them to make more use of the effective one-act farce.[8]

1. Feb. 17, 4:5.
2. March 17, 4:5.
3. May 5, 5:1.
4. Sept. 9, 4:6.
5. Sept. 28, 5:1.
6. Sept. 15, 4:5.
7. Oct. 7, 4:6.
8. Oct. 31, 1:6.

At this point, the Times had celebrated its sixth anniversary, and the dramatic reviews were relatively well-established. Their scope had been defined; all the various phases of theatre life that came within their compass had been touched at least once, and most of them had become permanent parts of the critiques. During the next few years, there are relatively few major changes in the content of the reviews and in their quality; I have recorded none at all for 1858 and 1859. A review of Boucicault's "The Colleen Bawn," produced in 1860 at Laura Keene's theatre, is fairly typical of the level that the criticism had then attained; it summarizes the plot, criticizes the plot development and the frequent changes of scenery which it entailed, lists the cast with some piquant, usually laudatory remarks about each major actor, notes the general effect of the production, and then goes into some detail about Boucicault's dramatic powers, particularly his power to write exciting and effective dialogue.[1] The production was better than the average theatrical fare of that day, even though it was not outstanding; and for a production of that kind, this type of review seems to me to be perfectly satisfactory. Certainly, anyone who reads this article in the Times to get an idea of the play he was going to see, or who wanted to find some criterion by which he could decide whether to visit Laura Keene's theatre or not, probably found in it adequate answers to his problem, and thus the primary function of drama criticism in the daily newspapers appears to have been fulfilled. I doubt that the dramatic reviews of today vary in any essentials from this review of "The Colleen Bawn," and it was certainly typical for the remainder of the period under study. For example, a review of Tom Taylor's "The Ticket-of-Leave Man," coming some three years later, followed pretty nearly the same pattern. It gave a quick sketch of the plot, discussed the characterization simultaneously with the acting, lauded the playwright this time not for his dialogue but for his creation of "powerful situations," and singled out, for special praise, the moral of the play and the scenery.[2] If such reviews, then, are accepted as typical, it seems natural to single out for discussion for the remaining years only those reviews which are outstandingly good, unusually poor or in any other way atypical.

The first of these is of particular interest when one tries to correlate the critics' and the public's opinions of stage performances.

1. 1860, Oct. 31, 8:1.
2. 1863, Dec. 3, 8:2.

Lester Wallack's "Rosedale" had been condemned by the critics almost unanimously as a rather feeble effort, yet night after night it continued to attract large crowds to the theatre, and much of Wallack's fame still rests on his performance in this play. After it had run for about three months, the Times' critic felt impelled to remark:

> The unchecked career of 'Rosedale' during the past three months has, in a way, placed this establishment beyond the pale of criticism. We have not thought it necessary to assail the work because it was a success. . . . The critic has the first say on the subject of a new play — the public the last. . . . The carpers have been silenced, and the play has continued to draw.[1]

The next unusual occurrence in this department of the Times was its failure to do anything unusual with the two most important theatrical events of the era: the performance of "Julius Caesar" with the three Booths, and the one-hundred-night run of Edwin Booth's "Hamlet."

The "Julius Caesar" was briefly announced on November 25, 1864.[2] On the following day, the amusement column did not even list the event, but was devoted in its entirety to a review of the opera "Don Sebastian." On November 27, a Sunday, there was no dramatic review at all, but there was a brief reference to the fire which had occurred at the Winter Garden during the performance of "Julius Caesar." The review was finally printed on November 29; it was only sixty-eight lines long, and was far below the level of criticism attained in the review of "The Colleen Bawn," let alone Swinton's critiques of Rachel. "Friday night was a night of triumph for the Winter Garden. The occasion was the great Booth benefit for the Shakespeare statue in the Central Park . . ." The rest of the first paragraph described the immense crowds jamming into the theatre, the fabulous admission prices, and the notables in the audience. The second paragraph discussed the performance:

> It is not usual to criticize performances on such occasions. Were it so, the critic would have, in this instance, a most agreeable task. It was in every respect admirable . . . the individual characteristic of Mr. Junius Booth, as exhibited in the performance of last night, seemed to us a careful conception and vigorous execution; that of Mr. Edwin Booth, a certain classic beauty and schollarly [*sic*] refinement which mark all his

1. 1863, Dec. 18, 4:4.
2. 4:5.

impersonations, and that of Mr. John Wilkes Booth, an *elan* and fire which at times fairly electrifies the audience and whirls them along with him.

The last paragraph briefly noted the enthusiastic response of the audience, and the receipts for the benefit. That was all.[1]

It is fairly obvious what had happened. The critic had written his review on the night of the performance for publication in the next morning's edition — hence the inadvertent use of "last night" instead of "Friday night" in the section quoted above — but lack of space had delayed its publication for four days. The lack of space was probably due to the fact that the performance came when the Civil War was drawing to its close, and immediately after Lincoln had been elected for a second term, so that the political news had an absolute priority.

The identical situation occurred with "Hamlet," with the single exception that the review appeared in the Times immediately after the play opened. The opening night fell on Saturday, November 26, and since, as I mentioned before, no theatrical reviews at all were printed on Sundays at that time, the review appeared on Monday, November 28. It ran to a scant total of thirty-two lines:

> Mr. Edwin Booth commenced his regular engagement at the Winter Garden on Saturday evening. The house was, of course, crowded, and the favor of its occupants was liberally bestowed upon the young and excellent tragedian. Shakespeare's 'Hamlet' was played, Mr. Booth sustaining the part of the Prince — a part in which he has no living equal. We have frequently dwelt upon its manifold merits, and need only add, on the present occasion, that each new performance reveals fresh traces of persistent study, of intellectual command, and of emotional sensibility. The play was in all respects well acted. It is seldom that we have a cast so substantially good, and we have no recollection of a Shakespearean revival that was more carefully and liberally undertaken. The scenery and dresses were entirely new and of a remarkable excellence. Messrs. Thorne and Witham — the artists — achieved a success that was justified by correctness and an eminent sense of the picturesque. The last-named gentleman is new to the city. His ability — like that of his associate — will speedily recommend him to the sympathies of the public. The expenditure for scenery is often extravagant, but it is seldom that we find, as in this instance, liberality and good taste so happily combined. Mr. Stuart has the unquestionable credit of producing 'Hamlet' in the best way it has yet been produced in New York. We can do no more at present than thus briefly refer to an art revival which is destined, we think, to be the sensation of the season. It is pleasant to know that a sensation can be directed into so worthily [*sic*] a channel.[2]

1. 5:1.
2. 4:5.

While this review is reasonably enthusiastic, and does emphasize
certain aspects of the presentation worthy of particular mention,
it really fails to present anything like an adequate picture of it.
Nor was this fault corrected later, when the production indeed became a "sensation." The first reference to it after this review appears in a Monday summary of events, on December 26: ". . . Mr.
Booth's *Hamlet* has fairly electrified the town. He has given it
twenty-four times, and the tragedy with its beautiful scenery, seems
destined to run for several weeks to come . . ."[1] (The scenery,
if nothing else, seems to have captured the critic's imagination.)
No notice of the play appears from that date on until March 22,
1865, the day on which the production was to terminate. To that
event, the one-hundredth performance, the Times devoted ten lines:

> WINTER GARDEN – BENEFIT OF EDWIN BOOTH. – This evening,
> Mr. Edwin Booth completes his one hundredth night of the performance
> of Hamlet, and takes his only benefit. This is a triumph, which, as the
> advertisements very justly state, reflects as much honor on the city
> whose good taste and refined perception has carried it to this, as on the
> genius of Mr. Booth who achieved it. The house will, of course, on such
> an occasion, be such as worthily to crown such an unequalled engage-
> ment.[2]

This is the typical notice run on the eve of an outstanding event.
The reader who, however, expected to find on the following day a
full-length description of the event, with a well-deserved eulogy
for Booth, was disappointed: this notice was the last mention of
the event in the Times. Such negligence is difficult to understand
even when the overwhelmingly important political news at just this
time is given its due consideration – the Times should have accorded to the "Julius Caesar" and the "Hamlet" an amount of
space comparable to that bestowed on Rachel some ten years
earlier.

Such shortcomings should not detract, however, from the value
of the reviews as a whole. The spirit of dramatic reform, evident
before in the demand for more realism in the acting and the plays,
is voiced again in a revolt against the spectacle-melodramas so popular at this time: "The theatrical tendency of the present day is
toward effect, action; and a rapid succession of brilliant scenes and
costumes are accepted as accomplishing all that the manager requires. The literary merit of a piece is now of little consequence
. . ."[3] And the need for morality on the stage is stressed again,

1. 5:1.   2. 4:5.
3. Review of Fisk's "Corporal Cartouche" at the Winter Garden, 1865, March 28,
4:5.

in a review of Mme. Ristori's performance of Alfieri's "Myrrah," at the French Theatre:

> Of course, Myrrah is not the sort of girl whom women care to see upon the stage, and however great may be its merits, a dramatic poem which does not please the female portion of the audience rarely goes flown with the public. . . . Nevertheless, nothing that can be alleged against 'Myrrah' as a play, should detract from our admiration of Mme. Ristori's fine acting.[1]

The following year — 1868 — saw Mrs. Scott-Siddons' debut in New York, an event which was handled expertly by the Times' critic. The play, "Romeo and Juliet," received only passing mention in the article which was one-third of a column long; the rest was devoted to a brief review of the actress' career and a detailed discussion of her acting technique — her entrances and exits, her use of facial expressions and gestures, and the like.[2] Three days later, the play was again reviewed; this time the emphasis was on the staging and on the adaptation of the text, and on Shakespearean revivals in New York in general, which, the critic asserted, result ". . . from a general sentiment for a better order of play than we have recently been . . . witnessing. The sensational drama has had its day. Its garish effects and twaddling dialogue have at length palled on the public appetite."[3] During the same season, the burlesque was vehemently denounced in a one-half-column article prompted by the large number of burlesques and extravaganzas then produced by most of the New York theatres:

> [Burlesques consist of] . . . a singular and easily detected mass of light and golden hair . . . a tendency in the [actresses] to dispossess themselves of their clothing . . . a series of piercing screams called comic singing, distorted and incoherent ravings called puns, and finally, strong convulsions denominated break-downs and walk-arounds. . . . The burlesque is . . . dangerous to dramatic art because it defies criticism. It is folly to weigh the merits of a pun — the strength of rival feminine heels and toes — and those graces of the human form which ought to be concealed from promiscuous gaze. Art has little, if anything, to do with the success of such entertainments.[4]

1. 1867, Oct. 1, 5:1.
2. Dec. 1, 4:7.
3. Dec. 4, 4:6.
4. 1869, Feb. 5, 5:2.

When the Waverley Theatre opened, during the same season, the critic found no novelty in either the theatre itself or the burlesques it showed except for "the fresh faces they present. Each is as pretty as paint can make it."[1] It is interesting to note that these attacks on the burlesque are based both on its alleged immorality and on its lack of literary or artistic merit. Yet the popularity of the burlesques continued, and occasionally the critic had to resign himself to reviewing them just as though they were productions more worthy of his attention. Thus the spectacle "The Twelve Temptations," presented at the Grand Opera House during the next season, was given almost a full column review, which discussed in considerable detail and without too much sarcasm the total lack of imagination, humor and plot in the spectacle, but praised its elaborate scenery and costumes as well as the beauty of its girl performers.[2]

By now, apparently, the popularity of Boucicault's plays had waned considerably, for during this season there appeared a rather outspoken review of Boucicault's "Lost at Sea," produced at Wallack's, which read in part:

> Mr. Boucicault is a consummate master of a certain kind of stage effect . . . but he is so tawdry, so stagy, and, except in his moments of highest inspiration, so intellectually commonplace, that his dramatic pabulum is apt to clog upon the taste, and to make one wish . . . for more matter and less art.

"Lost at Sea," with its barren plot and barren characterization, but its sensational fire scene, was cited as a typical example of Boucicault's dramatic output as a whole,[3] and the critic's opinion certainly seems to concur with the consensus of Boucicault's critics today.

The last of the three decades under study saw the rise of the "new" drama, chiefly through the productions of the plays of Tom Robertson and Gilbert; at the same time, the new, more realistic style of producing the classics, preeminently Shakespeare, was crystallized, and the opposition to the at best mediocre plays of the middle of the century grew enormously. The reviews in the Times, naturally, reflected all three phases of this development; the critique of Frederic Marsden's "Otto, a German," performed at the Broadway in 1878, is fairly typical of the reaction to the old-style German

1. Feb. 21, 5:1.
2. 1870, March 11, 5:5.
3. March 1, 5:4. A warning about the very real danger that this fire scene entailed appeared on March 10, 4:7.

comedy: It ". . . was produced . . . for the first time, and, we should be happy to add, for the last time . . . It is a trashy mixture of villainy, virtue, and vice, shaken in the ordinary manner, and administered *pianissimo*. But enough of the play; may it be the last of its race."[1]

This same reaction against the "old" drama manifested itself, perhaps more subtly, in the reception of Boucicault's plays during the late Seventies, and in the lack of enthusiasm for his acting engagement at the Booth Theatre in 1879. The Times' critic called the production of "The Colleen Bawn," with Boucicault and his wife, "a revival of memories rather than a serious undertaking," and expressed much the same sentiment toward a revival of "Arrah-na-Pogue."[2] More derogatory in a review of Boucicault's "Spell-Bound," at Wallack's, the critic hinted that such a production might indicate a decline in the management's standards.[3]

The "new" drama was widely hailed. Gilbert's "Pygmalion and Galatea," produced at Wallack's in 1872, was enthusiastically received; the Times' critic emphasized particularly its originality in mixing the fantastic with the realistic, its original approach to the theatre, and its humor, so far removed from the standard farce of the Fifties, and from the social comedies of later playwrights such as Daly.[4] Precisely the same qualities were praised when Gilbert's "Engaged" was produced at the Park Theatre in 1879, with particular stress on Gilbert's ability to present "improbabilities from a probable point-of-view."[5] But the native American drama — when it was original rather than adapted from British or French sources — found an almost higher praise, sometimes, as in the case of Bronson Howard's "The Banker's Daughter," based not on its intrinsic merits so much as on the very fact that it was both native and original:

UNION SQUARE THEATRE

The production of a successful American play at this theatre is an event in which every native dramatist is directly interested; for such a success must be regarded as a notable encouragement to dramatic art in this country, besides being one of the undoubted signs of the time. We are, in consequence, unusually happy to chronicle the emphatic success of Mr. Bronson Howard's new play, 'The Banker's Daughter,' which

1. Nov. 5, 4:7.
2. 1879, Feb. 11, 5:1; Feb. 12, 5:5.
3. Feb. 25, 5:4.
4. 1872, Oct. 4, 5:1.
5. Feb. 18, 5:3.

was represented for the first time last evening, and received with the most striking demonstrations of favor. . . . The generally accredited opinion that dramatic art, in this part of the world, can be at best but a stunted growth, is one of those superficial views which are upheld by the ignorance or superciliousness of a certain class of critics who, we are sorry to say, are only in too great number. The time will certainly come, however — and that period is not far off — when managers, public and critics will begin to perceive that domestic talent can produce fine work when it is sensibly encouraged, and that to delay such encouragement is to deprive ourselves of that which we have long endeavored to possess. . . .

The rest of this review, which occupied a full column, discussed the play at great length, going into its plot, its motivation and the major weaknesses of the motivation and characterization, its comic characters, the acting and the scenery.[1]

Finally, the transition to the "new" theatre manifested itself in the reviews of Shakespearean plays performed during the late Seventies, partly through the new views on the style of acting, and partly through the critics' own break with the traditional, romantic conception of Shakespeare. As to the style of acting, it is difficult to determine what the critics sought — they had evidently broken with the school of rant and bombast, but were, at the same time, unwilling to accept the moderns. The Times' critic who reviewed "Henry V" as produced at the Booth Theatre in 1875 was most disgruntled about the modern trends:

> . . . There are not many actors left in these days who can play one of Shakespeare's great parts, or even recite the lines properly. The 'artists' of the new school only know how to drawl out their words and stick their hands in their pockets. Mr. Rignold has evidently studied in a different school — it is a pleasure to hear him repeat the noble lines of Shakespeare, and his appearance and manners increase the effect of his declamation.[2]

The critic who reviewed Edwin Booth's engagement in 1878 — evidently a different person.[3] — took a directly antithetical view. The reviews of this engagement are, in my opinion, dramatic criticism in the press at its possible best, combining a detailed, informative analysis of a current production with a virtually scholarly discussion and interpretation of the play itself, and correlating the two with maximum effectiveness. At the same time, they exemplify clearly the rise of the new theatre, and, as I said before, the new

1. 1878, Dec. 1, 7:1.
2. Apr. 5, 4:7.
3. Probably Montgomery.

conception of Shakespeare which was beginning to take hold. They were published each time during this season that Booth offered a new Shakespearean play; I have selected three not because they were better than the others — all seem equally good — but because these three are, perhaps, the most typical. The first reviewed the performance of "Hamlet" which opened the engagement; it began with a quasi-apology, in which the critic pointed out that Booth's Hamlet was superb because the actor seemed to have "really disappeared in the character," but that admiration for his acting did not preclude disagreement with Booth's interpretation of the character. Whereupon, after citing Schlegel's famous utterance on the divergence of opinion on this subject, the critic proceeds to disagree:

> . . . Mr. Booth's Hamlet . . . has one vital weakness . . . an utter lack of emotional interest. . . . The heart is as fully apparent as the mind in this most complex of Shakespearean creations, and . . . its 'enormous intellectuality,' to borrow one of Coleridge's expressions, has been altogether too much insisted upon.

He briefly describes some earlier conceptions of the weak, intellectual, ivory-tower Hamlet — Goethe's, Schlegel's and Hazlitt's — and quotes the more modern, more realistic views of Professor Dowden; then he outlines his own conception:

> *Hamlet* is a man who feels deeply and thinks deeply; heart and mind are equally strong within him; he is brave, but keenly sensitive; he deems himself called to perform a terrible deed, against which his heart revolts; he is not troubled by cowardice, but . . . by scruples of conscience. . . . A weak man could never have undertaken what *Hamlet* overtook. . .

The rest of the review contrasts this view of Hamlet with Booth's interpretation.[1]

Three days later, a similar exposition formed the major part of a review of "Othello."

> Last evening at this [the Fifth Avenue] theatre, 'Hamlet' gave way to 'Othello,' with Mr. Booth as *Iago* and Mr. D. H. Harkins as the Moor. Mr. Booth's *Iago* is one of the most repulsive in the whole range of the drama, and yet, strange to say, it is more than endurable, it is fascinating. . . . Looked upon as a mere type of villainy, a 'demi-devil,' as Othello calls him, he is a conception out of all harmony with true art. But he is something different from this; he represents a great poetic creation, and despite the enormity of his wickedness, we are fain to listen to his words, which are impregnated with a most subtle harmony. He is a demon, if you will; but he is also a philosopher and a poet, and, let us add, a great character. Most actors picture him as a colloquial schemer and

1. Nov. 12, 5:5.

murderous cynic . . . they are unable to embody the general motive
which leads him to act as he does; to such false representations may be
traced that popular, but superficial, criticism, which declares that *Iago*
has no reason for his deeds.   But Mr. Booth conceives the character in
the right spirit. He pictures *Iago's* wickedness in all its enormity; but
he also embodies the inner nature of the man, wresting from him, as it
were, the secret of his uttermost thought and feeling . . . he is also a
marvel of grace, of insidiousness, of ripe intelligence; even we — against
our sympathies — are inclined to repeat the words which are addressed
to him by those whom he most deceives — 'honest Iago.' In short, Mr.
Booth's conception of *Iago* is all that Shakespeare imagined him to
be. . .[1]

On the next night, Booth and Harkins again performed "Othello,"
but switched their parts, not too successfully. Harkins, on the pre-
vious night, could not have been (and, by the critics' consensus, was
not) a worthy match for Booth, even though he is said to have been
a good actor; but playing Iago on the night following Booth's ren-
dering of the same role with any degree of success was impossible.
At the same time, Booth was apparently a better Iago than an
Othello. According to the Times' critic, Booth failed in this im-
personation for two reasons: He was unable ". . . to express the
highest notes of tragic emotion and passion . . ." especially in the
scene in which Othello is first made aware of Desdemona's alleged
faithlessness; "his rage is powerful but not thrilling." And at the
same time, Booth was not sufficiently natural in the love scenes;
the critic describes him as cold and too studied where he should be
understanding, yielding and tender, particularly in the final scene
of the play, for ". . . *Othello* is less a brute and more a man. If
Othello were the unsympathetic savage, as depicted by others . . .
we could find no philosophical reason for the love which *Desdemona* gives him freely."[2]

These reviews, coming at the very end of the period under study,
are certainly far removed in content, in form, in style, and in inher-
ent critical acuteness, from the notice of the Bateman children's
"Richard III" with which this survey began. And it seems to me
that this development of dramatic criticism in the Times is more
than the progress of one department in one newspaper, but that, at
the same time, it mirrors the progress of the entire metropolitan theatrical world of those years — without true foresight, without true
perspective, without true objectivity, but with a huge amount of
infinitesimal detail, made most useful by the comment and opinions

1. Nov. 15, 5:3.
2. Nov. 16, 5:1.

of contemporary figures inside this theatrical world.

Some of this information comes from articles which are not, strictly speaking, dramatic reviews, but which are closely enough related to the reviews to warrant inclusion here. Among these are primarily forecasts of coming and summaries of past theatre seasons, editorials, and a limited number of feature articles.

The end-of-season summaries are generally of little interest, except perhaps as brief, convenient surveys, but even as those they are ordinarily too superficial to merit close attention. They appeared regularly every year, but varied in length from three lines to well over a column. The forecasts, which usually appeared in the last week of August or the first week of September, are considerably more valuable, since they note the opening of new theatres, innovations in theatres, changes in management and new members of acting companies.[1] The forecast for the season of 1855-1856 included a survey of the theatres' financial status; possibly it reflects the growing economic troubles of New York which culminated in the great panic of 1857.[2] A rather unusual forecast was published in June of 1866:

> The Summer season commenced last evening at many places and in many ways. It is difficult, now, to know where or when any season ends. A few years since the lines were more clearly defined. From the middle of May until the first week of September there was nothing that the critic or the public need regard. Mr. Stuart broke through this placid and agreeable state of affairs by giving a Summer season at the old Wallack Theatre . . . ever since we have been favored with 'seasons' by all the other theatrical establishments of New York.

A brief listing of that summer's offerings followed.[3]

Special feature articles on the theatre appeared infrequently — I found only seventeen for the entire period, which were chiefly concerned with the stage — but they do cover almost the whole range of it, and frequently give information not contained in the reviews. Only one such article deals with a playwright; it is an extended biographical sketch of Joanna Baillie, which appeared in the second issue of the Times as part of a series called "Limnings of Literary People, With Some 'Pencillings' of Painters and Players."[4] On the foreign stage, I found only one article, again, called "The

---

1. For example: Wallack's, 1853, Sept. 8, 4:4; Burton's 1854, Sept. 7, 4:4; Laura Keene's Varieties, 1857, Sept. 1, 4:6; Wallack's, 1862, Sept. 20, 2:5.

2. Sept. 15, 4:3.

3.. June 4, 4:7.

4.. 1851, Sept. 19, 2:5. Unless otherwise stated, all these articles are anonymous.

Drama in Germany"; it deals at length with the new plays being written at the time, and discusses, more briefly, the German actors' style in representing both modern and classic plays.[1]   One article deals with a specific play — Sheridan's "The Rivals"; it appeared while the play was being presented at Wallack's, and while Burton was preparing a production of it at the Chambers Street Theatre.[2] An article — rather, a series of notes — on the dramatization of novels appeared in 1855, prompted by the popularity, at that time, of Burton's and Brougham's adaptations of Dickens' novels.[3]

Several articles dealt with specific actors. The first of these summarized and discussed an article on Tyrone Power which had appeared in an unidentified Dublin magazine,[4] the next, appearing only a few days later, dealt with current performances by children, mainly the Batemans.[5]   During the same year, the Times published a series of anecdotes about Edwin Booth.[6]   The last of these articles on individual actors appeared much later, on the occasion of John Gilbert's fiftieth anniversary on the stage; it discussed not only his career, but the style of his acting as well.[7]

C. L. Brace ("C. L. B.") devoted one article in his then popular series, "Walks Among the New York Poor," to a description of the street urchins and "vagrant youths" who filled the "pit" at the National Theatre on Chatham Street; the article is vaguely reminiscent of Dekker's description of an Elizabethan audience in *The Gull's Horn-Book*. Brace's article makes this lower-class audience in a lower-class theatre fairly come to life, with peanuts crunching, beer-bottles popping, sandwich-bags rattling, and a great deal of noisy participation in the stage performance.[8]   The only other article on theatre audiences is in sharp contrast to this one — it is the highly satirical description of the audience in the Academy of Music at Rachel's opening performance in 1855 which I mentioned earlier.

Several articles are devoted to the state of the theatre and the quality of productions in general. The first, matter-of-factly called "The Way Plays Are Produced in Some Places," describes the cos-

1. 1873, Dec. 13, 4:5.
2. 1852, Sept. 27, 1:5.
3. 1855, Jan 17, 4:4.
4. 1852, Oct. 1, 6:1.
5. Oct. 5, 1:3.
6. Dec. 6, 7:1.
7. 1878, Dec. 2, 5:3.
8. 1853, Jan 21, 2:3.

tumes, scenery and stage "props" then in use at New York's most
popular theatres, mainly Wallack's, Burton's and the Broadway;
the last third of this one-and-a-half column article quotes an article on Charles Kean's production of "Macbeth" from *Chambers'
Journal*, which deals largely with Kean's new method of staging.[1]
When Laura Keene opened her Variety Theatre, the Times devoted
a one-half column article to a rather ironic description of the type
of "show" that she was planning to present.[2] On December 3,
1858, the leading article in the Times, occupying a full four of the
six front-page columns, was called "Our City Amusements, How
the Mass of the People Amuse Themselves, By the Strong-Minded
Reporter of the New York Times," and began:

> In obedience to the Editor-in-Chief, I undertook to 'to go about' [*sic*]
> among the amusements, and describe such of them as were not habitually
> 'done up' under the regular head, in order that the readers of the TIMES
> might learn how the great mass of our People . . . secure that relaxation
> and amusement which seems a necessity for every class.

The article covers, with perhaps pardonable intellectual snob-
bery, all kinds of places of amusement other than the opera, concert halls and legitimate theatres: the circuses, the "museums" such
as Barnum's, the Bowery and National Theatres — "both places are
the select home of the melodrama of the blood-and-thunder school"
— and a place known as the "Model Artists," perhaps a forerunner
of our modern nightclubs, which was a huge saloon giving continu-
ous entertainment, chiefly by feminine variety performers. Each of
these places is treated in a separate section, and each section describes not only the attractions offered there, but the size and type
of audience attracted; the style of the "Strong-Minded Reporter,"
however, seems to me to fall far below that of C. L. Brace.

Ordinarily, the Times carried on its attack on the quality of productions in the legitimate theatres in its editorials; twice, however,
special articles were devoted to this campaign. One was a reply to
Barney Williams, who had, in a curtain speech at Niblo's, charged
the Times' critic with condemning Gayler's "Connie Soogah" and
similar plays merely because they were written by native Americans.
Though the chauvinism evident in many of the Times' reviews was
itself ample refutation, the Times reviewed its position in this article, and used the opportunity to deal some sound blows to Barney
Williams and the Irish Theatre in general. "The record of this par-

1. 1853, Apr. 30, 2:4.
2. 1855, Dec. 28, 4:5.

ticular sheet is clear. It has conscientiously, persistently and vehemently urged the just claims of Americans to the high places in
art . . . " but it has not supported all artists, just because they were
born in the United States. As for "Connie Soogah," the writer repeated the criticism made in the original review, that it was a play
written solely as a "vehicle" for the stars, and vigorously denounced
the "star system" as a whole. And as to the Irish Drama — "A
dreary quagmire of vile colloquialisms; a senseless chattering on the
part of one or two artists, and a mean subservience on the part of
every one else; a rancid humor of the whiskey-bottle . . . these are
its ingredients."[1]

The other article on the state of the theatre was called "The
Revival," and summarized clearly and concisely the views that the
critics had already expressed in the specific reviews:

> . . . theatrical matters, just now, are at a low ebb in the City. 'Humpty
> Dumpty,' which is pantomime, and 'Ixion,' which is burlesque, carry
> the town. But where drama pure and simple is played there is apathy. . . .
> The principal theatres . . . are barely making expenses, and none of them
> deserve to do so. . . .

Even the Shakespearean revivals in the various theatres are far below standard, since most of them serve merely as vehicles for individual stars.

> We need a revival on the part of the public of the quick, intelligent
> watchfulness which looks for intellect, not stupidity, on the stage. . . .
> which applauds the word, not the scene, and which, in fact, has some-
> thing more than eyes for a theatrical performance.[2]

The attack on the star system was pursued in another article, in
the same month, which condemned it for leading to the employment of incompetent actors in the supporting roles, evidently its
worst effect.[3]

Finally, there are three more isolated articles of more than casual
interest. One of these deals with matinees, which had been introduced for the first time about the middle of the Nineteenth Century.
The article charges that the managers were disguising these matinees
as dress rehearsals to which the public was admitted, in order to
present performances for which the actors would receive no pay
whatsoever, and denounces the utter carelessness and casualness

1. 1864, Jan. 18, 8:2. The review appeared Jan. 13, 4:4.
2. 1868, Dec. 7, 4:7.
3. Dec. 21, 4:7.

with which these matinees were both staged and acted.[1]   The
second — the only one of its kind which I was able to discover —
was a financial report on all the theatres for 1868, listing the annual revenue minus the two percent Federal tax for each establishment, and reporting a total revenue of 2,980,175 dollars for all
combined.[2]   The last is a one-column article called "Some Re-
flections on Old Play-Bills," which cites the earliest extant American playbill and discusses the development of playbills, as to content and make-up, from then on to date.[3]

There remain for discussion the editorials proper; and perhaps
the most amazing thing about them is their huge number. It is virtually impossible to treat them all individually; consequently, editorials dealing largely with musical affairs have been ignored, and
an attempt has been made to classify the others by general subject
matter. Their number cannot be over-emphasized; except for the
Civil War period, and during Presidential elections and similar political events, editorials on various theatrical matters appeared almost
weekly. In 1852, when the Times devoted more space to operas
and concerts than to the drama, three editorials on musical matters
appeared in May, and as many as six in June. During September,
1855, four separate editorials dealt with the Rachel engagement
alone. Almost equally striking as the sheer number of these editorials is their militancy, indicating perhaps that the theatre in those
days was much more a matter of public concern than it is today,
and showing, I think, most clearly that the press considered dramatic criticism as a responsibility, the faithful discharge of which
it most definitely owed to the public.

Some editorials merely summarized current stage events, or sur-
veyed events scheduled for coming seasons, without commenting
more than casually on their quality.[4]   Many more dealt specifi-
cally with the literary and moral — especially the moral — value of
current entertainment. The first of these appeared about the same
time as the first critical notice, defined the theatre's main purpose
as one of public instruction in morality by visual representation,
and proceeded to denounce the managers of the day as falling far
short of this aim.[5]   The next was called "City Amusements," and
began with a denunciation of operas as violating the medium of the

1. 1867, Sept. 23, 4:6.
2. 1869, Jan. 27, 4:7.
3. 1868, Nov. 1, 5:2.
4. For example, 1853, Feb. 17, 4:5; 1872, Sept. 13, 4:5.
5. 1852, Sept. 29, 4:2.

stage by failing to have the action conform to the dialogue; for example: "Two operatic noblemen quarrel . . . each declares that the other shall 'the next moment die.' They, however, mutually seem to consent to put off the execution of these threats in order to sing a duet . . ." The editorial proceeded to say that "Our legitimate plays are not much better" because they foster conventional, unnatural action. "Attitude and 'points' are hereditary on the stage, albeit, in almost every instance, the attitude is stilted and the 'points' unnatural." It cited the efforts of a German acting company in London to break through these conventions, and went on to say:

> Our City amusements — particularly theatrical — must strike the stranger as very defective. In no city in the world have managers and actors so much license as here. No censorship of the press exists. Grossness and indelicacy on the stage are permitted to go unpunished, poverty of decoration and scenery is submitted to patiently by the public and . . . seldom is there that proper care and attention to the detail and effect which a cultivated people have a right to expect.

Negligence in costumes, staging and scenery — anachronisms and the like — are defeating not only the pleasure to be derived from the theatre, but its educational aspects as well. The rest of the editorial is devoted to the promise of more careful criticism which I quoted earlier.[1]

The editorial campaign for better entertainment was then carried to specific presentations, first with a violent denunciation of the animal performances at the Hippodrome,[2] and next with a eulogy on the public reaction to the dramatization of *Uncle Tom's Cabin*, at the National Theatre:

> For the first time, with one or two indifferent exceptions, in the history of our stage, piety and morality are found to play in . . . the theatre. The event may mark a new era in dramatic representation in this country.

Generally, the editorial continues, the theatre has been a bad moral influence, despite its sponsorship by the intellectual elite; most theatres, "through want of legitimate income," are corrupt, so that they present only coarse and vulgar plays, and increase their revenue by selling liquor during the performance and permit prostitutes to solicit business in the theatre lobbies.[3]

1. 1853, Jan. 17, 4:3
2. May 16, 4:3
3. Oct. 25, 4:2.

The next editorial is a vehement indictment of P. T. Barnum for defrauding the public with "fake" entertainment, and, even more, for admitting these frauds in his autobiography and excusing them with the statement that the public likes to be deceived.[1] The morality of stage performances is the subject of another editorial, written on the occasion of a speech by the Reverend Dr. Bellows defending the theatres.[2] The Civil War period abruptly halted the campaign, but soon afterwards the fight was taken up again, with two successive editorials on such disreputable shows as most spectacles, ballets and burlesques, and the then new type of performance known as "opera bouffe."[3] The ballet was the target of another editorial in this series one-and-a-half years later.[4]

Many editorials, however, were concerned with aspects of the theatre other than its alleged lack of morality. One condemns the "free adaptations" from French plays as literary piracy;[5] another comments on the "heroic revival" on the occasion of a Paris production of de Bornier's classic drama "La Fille de Roland";[6] another discusses the causes for France's eminence in dramatic literature, and briefly reviews the history of the drama since the fifteenth century in France, England, Spain and Germany.[7] The list of editorials and of the subjects they treat seems unending. Joseph Jefferson is severely criticized for restricting his talent to a single play;[8] Boucicault is ridiculed for boasting publicly of his genius.[9] Another group of editorials deals with ills in the production of plays and the construction of theatres: one asks the architects to provide for better ventilation,[10] and another, after reviewing trends in costuming since the Elizabethan era, charges that the use of modern dress on the stage leads actresses to spending a great deal of money on their dresses to "show off" before the public and outdo their rivals, and also leads toward situations where actresses portraying women in dire financial distress will appear onstage in a Parisian creation worth several hundred dollars.[11]

I have already mentioned that the Times' editors joined the cam-

1. 1854, Dec. 16, 4:2.
2. 1857, May 1, 4:4.
3. 1868, Nov. 8, 4:4.
4. 1870, March 20, 4:4.
5. 1874, Feb. 1, 4:5.
6. 1875, March 11, 6:5.
7. 1879, Feb. 23, 6:5.
8. 1877, Oct. 26, 4:5.
9. 1873, Dec. 13, 6:6.
10. 1857, May 4, 4:5.
11. 1875, Apr. 16, 4:4.

paign against the high admission prices charged by the Academy of Music during the Rachel engagement. There were altogether three editorials on this subject;[1] and, after the joint action by the press and the ever-declining attendance had forced Rachel's manager to lower the prices, a fourth editorial in the Times deplored the lateness of the action.[2] Aside from these, I found two other editorials dealing with the finances of the theatres; one treated in general terms the box office receipts of operatic and theatrical establishments in 1858,[3] and the other discussed the bankruptcy of Buckstone's Haymarket Theatre in London in 1871, comparing the financial success of Wallack's.[4]

The last group of editorials is probably the largest, and, for this work, probably the most interesting, for it deals with dramatic criticism as such. The first of this group discusses the critical standards on the New York *Courier;*[5] the next, after denouncing the New York *Mirror* for unfairly criticizing the musician William Henry Fry, urges the adoption of definite standards for the dramatic and musical critics of the press.[6] Two months later, an editorial on the operatic engagement of Mme. Sontag vehemently opposes the use of a performer's past success in Europe, or of the attendance record at his performances, as criteria for criticism.[7]

In 1853, Burton became involved in a violent dispute with William Young, the editor of the *Albion*, and the Times published their correspondence in this dispute. Young had apparently criticized some of Burton's performances, and Burton, riled beyond endurance, wrote a letter to the Times charging that Young was merely avenging Burton's rejection of a play that Young had written. Young, in turn, published a letter by Burton showing that the play in question had not been rejected at all. The controversy filled the letter column in the Times for several days, until a Times editorial finally put an end to it:

> . . . this explosion is the result of a system which has long been gaining ground in this City, and which is entirely opposed to the traditional prerogative attached to the press. It means, in plain language, that independent criticism has no right to exist in any form, save that which is pleasing to the proprietors of the theatres. It means that managers

1. 1855, Sept. 6, 4:3; Sept. 8, 4:3; Sept. 13, 4:1.
2. Sept. 21, 4:2.
3. 1858, Dec. 9, 4:5.
4. 1871, May 14, 4:3.
5. 1852, Oct. 1, 4:5.
6. 1852, Nov. 23, 4:4.
7. 1853, Feb. 11, 4:3.

believe that any newspaper in which they advertise their performances, is bound to notice their establishment favorably. It means that, if the critic blames what is blameable, he is liable to exclusion from the theatre, or to an attack in the public prints, or, perhaps, to an assault less legal and manly. . . .

Everyone knows what a powerful agent the stage may become for the destruction of morality. . . . Nor have we . . . very strong faith in the converse of this proposition. The stage may be the source of much evil, but it can never, under any circumstances, be converted into a stimulus, of any great power, to virtue. The most that can be done with it, is to gratify it into an innocent recreation; out of this arose the necessity that created the theatrical critic. . . . To discharge this duty properly, it was of the highest importance that the critic be an independent channel of communication. . . . The theatrical critic is therefore . . . chosen . . . as being a man of correct taste and dramatic experience. . . . A manager, it seems to us, has no right to deny a critic's right to give an adverse decision . . . the open position in which he voluntarily places himself cuts him off from all appeal or retaliation. . . . He is a caterer for the public amusement, and has no right to grumble at being publicly judged.[1]

A clearer, more careful definition of the critics' tasks and their relation to the theatre managers can hardly be imagined. Strangely enough, during the same year, the Times itself became involved in a controversy very similar to the Burton-Young dispute. On November 24, the Times reviewed Burton's production of Boucicault's "The Fox Hunt"; it was a fairly satirical review which praised the dialogue and the acting, but denounced the plot for being too involved and being not original, as the advertisements claimed, but really an adaptation of a French comedy called "Sullivan."[2] A letter by Boucicault to the Times, published two days later, took strong exception to this last point, renewing the claim of originality. The Times appended an editorial note which

. . . would remind Mr. Boucicault that an article written between the time of leaving a theatre and the period of going to press will not . . . permit extraordinary caution and investigation. The critic must seize on the obvious points, and weigh them to the best of his ability. Only those he can deal with. Investigation results . . . when it is demanded.[3]

This sounded very much like an advance retraction and apology, as though the editors did not have much confidence in their critic. But on November 30, apparently after some thorough "investigation," the Times' critic published a reply to Boucicault, repeating his charge and documenting it with quotations from specific scenes

1. 1853, March 28, 4:3.
2. 4:4.
3. 4:3.

from both plays as well as with a scene-by-scene plot outline.[1]
On the next day, Boucicault replied again, denying any similarity
between the two plays except in one scene, challenging the Times
to submit both plays to literary judges, and alleging that the Times
was refusing to admit an obvious error.[2]   This last, evidently
rather arrogant statement, was a tactical mistake which the Times
was quick to seize upon: the leading news story on the following
day, and an editorial, vigorously rejected Boucicault's challenge
and accused him of being a poor loser as well as "rather less than a
gentleman."[3]   Boucicault apparently thought the whole matter
over for a few days, and decided that he was foolish to risk the
favor of the Times, till then rather liberally bestowed; and so he
wrote a carefully worded letter in which he did not admit to plagiarism, but did apologize for casting asperions on the integrity of
the Times.   The editors appended a self-satisfied note to his letter,
and there the matter ended.[4]

This controversy serves, I think, as a practical demonstration of
the principles of dramatic criticism outlined in the earlier editorial;
it shows, at the same time, that the Times vigorously participated
in such matters editorially, rather than leaving, as though with de-
tachment, the onus of the battle to the harassed critic.   Once more
that year, the Times took up the fight for fair aesthetic criticism
in the press; this time it was an attack on the New York *Herald*,
the Times' perennial foe, for misusing the privilege of critique to
ruin an operatic enterprise started by the unfortunate Mr. Fry.[5]

There are two more editorials on the subject of criticism which
are worthy of note. One, "The Real Dramatic Critic," discusses the
taste of the average theatre audience, its predilection for burlesque
and melodrama, its inability to "distinguish the highest merit" but
its refusal to, "as a rule, accept anything very bad."[6]   The other
defines the task of the music critic, but should be included here
since it unquestionably reflects the Times' attitude on criticism
as a whole.   The music critics of the press, the editorial stated,
". . . have a task, the delicacy and frequent irksomeness of which
is rarely appreciated by the public . . . and not at all by some of
those who are most needed . . . to their commendation, and . . . their

1. 1:3.
2. Dec. 1, 1:3.
3. 1:1; 4:2.
4. Dec. 5, 1:4.
5. Dec. 15, 4:1; Dec. 16, 1:3; Dec. 19, 4:3; Dec. 24, 4:1.
6. 1875, Apr. 22, 6:3.

forbearance." Both the managers and the performers consider the
critics' task as being solely that of praise and free advertising; they
look upon critics who find fault as public enemies. But ". . . musical criticisms properly written involve preparation, thought, and
self-sacrifice; and . . . they have a place in the art education of the
public." The self-sacrifice cannot be over-emphasized, since the
critic must necessarily shut out all personal preferences and preju-
dices in favor of the public interest; thus, for example, he must be
more lenient toward the moderns, since the public interest requires
that they be encouraged by the critics, even if their works are not
worthy of praise.[1]

Thus the whole scope of dramatic criticism on the Times from
the first issue to 1879 has been covered, even though not every review, not every editorial has been treated — a task which would
have exceeded the purpose of this work, and would probably have
been to a large extent unrewarding. There remains for discussion,
however, some material on the way in which the reviews were written. One phase of this material — the obstacles the critics met in
gaining access to the various presentations — has already been
touched upon in Part I; but there is other material, both explicit
in comment by outsiders and implied in the reviews themselves.
The New York *Dramatic News* considered dramatic criticism by
the press ineffective because the critics are allegedly prejudiced toward individual plays and actors, because they may be influenced
by the amount of advertising which a given theatre gave to a newspaper, and because they supposedly approached a play from an
"objective, intellectual" point of view rather than through "the
passions."[2] Boucicault considered criticism by the press imprac-
ticable: ". . . newspaper criticism of dramatic work is rendered impossible . . . [by] the conditions and necessities of the daily press.
The performance of a play . . . terminates at eleven o'clock. The
journalist must have his copy in the hands of the compositor by
half past twelve."[3] Winter, in an admitted reply to Boucicault,
cited a play for which a critic of the Times had written the review
". . . in my presence, after the fall of the last curtain. It nearly
filled one column. It was written in exactly forty minutes and it
could not have been better . . . if its author had worked on it for
forty days."[4] Later, Winter cited, again in defense of the critics,

1. 1878, Dec. 28, 6:3.
2. Vol. III, No. 5, 5:2 (Oct. 28, 1876).
3. "At the Goethe Society" (an address), *North American Review*, Vol. CXLVIII,
No. 338, p. 335 (March, 1889).
4. *The Press and the Stage*, p. 43.

the obstacles under which they had to work — "The weather, the crowds, the vile air, the haste, the anxiety, the midnight drudgery, the newspaper squabbles, the alienated friendships, the cackle of defamatory destruction . . ."[1]

The speed with which they had to write the reviews was probably the biggest single obstacle with which the critics had to cope. The other, less annoying only because it occurred less frequently, was the problem of more than one premiere on the same night. For both problems, the critics apparently devised the same solution, one that is both simple and satisfactory, and still, to some extent, in use today: They wrote a brief review covering mainly the plot of the play and its general impression on the night of the performance, and wrote a more extended review of the play at a later date. Of course, this did not happen always, or even with a majority of the plays reviewed, but it did occur with sufficient frequency to establish the existence of a definite trend. Thus, in a review of "Romeo and Juliet" at the Booth Theatre, the critic gave his general impression, briefly praised the scenery, the acting and the costumes, and continued: "But to these and cognate topics we must hereafter refer, our habit being not to write a column before breakfast on the day of the performance, and to insert a comma by the way of comment after supper."[2]   The same procedure was noted in a review of Tom Taylor's "Men and Acres," at Wallack's: "We for the present merely chronicle the . . . success . . . reserving the more extended notice for future publication."[3]

Not always, when there was more than one premiere on the same night, could the critic afford to postpone his reviews until a later date — after all, he had to at least catch a glimpse of the performances if he were to review them at all. In the early days, when there was apparently only one man available to cover these performances, the critic must have spent a nearly frantic evening. Thus, on September 6, 1853, the critic first visited a concert at the Castle Garden, then attended a variety performance at Niblo's Garden — "we were unable to witness the first selections" evidently because "we" had to attend the concert — and next went to see a comedy at Wallack's, but "other engagements interfered with our attendance in the early part of the evening. We arrived in time for Mr. Wallack's speech only."[4]

1. "The Critic," *The Actor and Other Speeches*, p. 30.
2. 1869, Feb. 4, 5:1.
3. 1870, Apr. 7, 5:3.
4. 4:5.

But that situation was soon remedied. When, later, more than one play opened during the same evening, the Times apparently sent some reporters, not needed for other assignments, out with the critic. Thus, on December 25, 1855, both Planche's "King Charming," at the Broadway, and Brougham's "Pocahontas," at Wallack's, received full-length reviews, and the style of the one review is so different from the other that two different persons must have covered the two plays.[1] The same technique was evidently used henceforth whenever this situation occurred.

I found only two general remarks on the dramatic reviews in the Times; and one of these is by the Times itself: ". . . matters connected with the Fine Arts have been discussed in . . . the Daily Times in a manner calculated to win the respect of artists and the public. As a critical journal, its position has been recognized."[2] The other appeared in *The Round Table*: "The musical and dramatic criticisms of the *Times* have been, we think, discriminating and just, leaning, perhaps . . . sometimes overmuch to praise — an error on the side of amiability which it is difficult to censure."[3]

This development of the art of dramatic criticism in the Times seems to me to be a valuable subject for study not only because the reviews reflect the progress of a newspaper in a given field, or even because they chronicle theatrical trends, but because the critics, through their reviews, unquestionably influence, and perhaps even, to a large extent, direct, the course of theatrical offerings in the city.

> That they have power all sides will agree. Critics are called critics mainly when they are writing dissents, and if there are nine bad notices in nine daily Manhattan newspapers, that play will not be selling out the following night. Further, there is a better than fair chance it will be closing Saturday. . . .[4]

1. 4:3.
2. Editorial, 1853, Dec. 24, 4:1.
3. "The American Press," No. II, "The Metropolitan Dailies," V, 327:3. (May 25, 1867).
4. Nichols, *op. cit.*, 17:4.

III

THE AUTHORSHIP OF THE REVIEWS

The dramatic reviews of the Times are not a mere mechanical recording of theatrical events; they are a running commentary of these events as well. Such a commentary reflects not only the broad social trends of the time and the general editorial policy of the newspaper, but also the personal views, and through them the personality and background, of the individual critic. It would be useful, therefore, to correlate the biographical material about the critics with the reviews they wrote, but such correlation is rendered impossible by the scarcity of biographical data, and by the infinitesimal number of reviews of which the authorship can be positively established.

Still, this study would hardly be complete without an attempt to identify the authors of at least some of the reviews. The major obstacle to such an attempt is, of course, the fact that all the reviews examined are anonymous. An almost equally great obstacle is the fact that the style of the reviews is largely set by newspaper usage, and that any individual characteristics of style may have been modified, no one knows to what extent, by editors and re-write men. Stylistic parallels are therefore dubious evidence as to authorship, and have been used only rarely here. The attempt to establish authorship must thus rely largely on what little external evidence is available, and is therefore confined to a very limited number of reviews.

The dates of the individual critic's employment by the Times lead mainly to negative conclusions. If, for example, the date on which a critic started to work for the Times is known, it can be concluded only that he did not write any reviews published before that date. It cannot be asserted that he wrote all the subsequent reviews, since almost throughout the period under study, several critics were working for the Times simultaneously; even during the years from 1872 to 1877, when Schwab is the only critic known to have been working for the Times, someone else, never identified, may have occasionally written the reviews. It is possible, however, to draw the following general conclusions from the length and consistency of the critics' connection with the Times:

1. Since Seymour was employed by the Times on a full-time basis, while his colleagues O'Brien, Swinton, Daly, Wilkins, Hurlbert and Leland were employed as critics on temporary or a free-lance basis only, it is probable that most of the reviews between 1852 and May 2, 1869 were written by Seymour.

2. During the summer of 1862, while Seymour was in London, the reviews were possibly written by Hurlbert, who had returned from Europe in 1861, although anyone else may have substituted for Seymour during these months.

3. During most of 1865, Seymour was writing for other publications, and so his authorship of the reviews in the Times during that year is doubtful. There is no hint, even, as to the person who may have written the Times' reviews in his stead; it may have been any of the critics then living.

4. From April to September, 1868, while Seymour was in Paris, the reviews were probably written by Daly.

5. From 1872 to 1877, most of the reviews were probably written by Schwab.

6. From 1877 to 1880, Schwab, who was mentioned more frequently as a music critic than as a drama critic, probably wrote few dramatic reviews; most of these, during this period, were probably written by Montgomery.

It is not safe to draw any more definite conclusions from the dates of employment. Most of the remaining data concerning the authorship of the reviews pertain to individual reviews rather than to whole periods of publication, and are, therefore, presented in the same order as the biographical material on the critics.

No one review can definitely be assigned to Fitz-James O'Brien. Professor Wolle suggests that since little is known of O'Brien's activities from August, 1853, to May, 1854, any of the musical or dramatic critiques in the Times during this period may be his;[1] however, Seymour was then writing reviews for the Times, and Remack may have been, so that this suggestion does not lead to any positive identification. Professor Wolle does, however, ascribe to O'Brien the review published at the end of the season of 1852-1853. This review stated in part: "During the past season Mr. Wallack has produced 18 leading pieces; 17 of them old, one new, and none origi-

1. *Op. cit.*, p. 30.

nal (if we except a farce produced on Christmas Eve)."[1] This farce was O'Brien's own "My Christmas Dinner"; Professor Wolle postu-lates that O'Brien must have written this review himself, "for no one but the author would single out as an exception, such a minor production."[2] For the same reason, Professor Wolle also assigns the review of O'Brien's "Duke Humphrey's Dinner"[3] to O'Brien himself.[4] These conclusions appear to be unsound. There were few "original" plays produced during the season of 1852-1853, so that any play with an original theme and an original plot would be outstanding even if it were otherwise a poor play. But even grant-ing that the review was prejudiced in O'Brien's favor, it is not nec-essarily true that O'Brien himself must therefore be the author. He was connected with the Times, and any of the Times' critics may have been inclined to review favorably a play by a colleague. At the same time, Seymour and O'Brien were close friends, through their association with Henry Clapp and the Bohemian circle, and, if Seymour reviewed O'Brien's play, he might also have been in-clined toward undue leniency and praise. And further: of O'Brien's six plays, two others were reviewed in the Times, and both, again, favorably;[5] and "The Gentleman from Ireland" was revived in 1869, eight years after O'Brien's death, and again widely acclaimed.[6] It seems, therefore, illogical to ascribe to O'Brien the reviews of his own plays merely because they happen to be favorable. Finally, the review of the premiere of "The Gentleman from Ireland" con-tains the statement that "The tag to the second act is perhaps a trifle too long . . . " a criticism which O'Brien would certainly not have made, had he written the review himself. The review also mis-spells his name – "O'Brian" – and describes at length his antics during the curtain calls; both of these circumstances point to a critic other than O'Brien. If this review is conceded to be by a critic other than O'Brien, why should he have reviewed his other plays himself?

None of O'Brien's other biographers and editors identifies any of his dramatic reviews; nor can any identifications be made by comparing the style of his short stories and his two known articles

1. 1853, June 14, 1:4.
2. *Op. cit.*, pp. 51-52.
3. 1856, Feb. 5, 4:2.
4. *Op. cit.*, p. 112.
5. "The Gentleman from Ireland," 1854, Dec. 12, 4:5; "The Sister," 1854, Dec. 28, 4:5.
6. Feb. 23, 5:3.

in the Times to the style of the reviews of this period. It should be pointed out, however, that while most of the reviews of the period are written in a sober, business-like, purely expository style, some few are written in a lighter, more satirical and perhaps even more facetious vein. It seems unlikely that both styles were used by the same critic; and if Seymour wrote the majority of the reviews, the less formal ones were probably written by someone else, possibly by O'Brien. I am rather hesitant in making this vague suggestion, even, since Seymour could be very satirical, and even somewhat facetious (as in his signed dispatches from London and Paris), so that he might easily be the author of both types of reviews. Still, the difference in style is very pronounced. Compare, for example, the review of Mrs. Centlivre's "Busy Body," which was quoted earlier, to the following:

> ...we...strolled into Mr. Wallack's pretty theatre. We confess to unalloyed gratification – a wondrous confession for a dramatic critic. Such persons are naturally fastidious. They have seen everything, heard everything, know everything. . . . They are desperately understanding in matters of costume, and have their wrath frequently excited by seeing the dresses of three distinct reigns all on the stage at once.[1]

Or:

> ...the literary antecedents of the author of this piece (Mr. A. Harris) did not lead us to hope for an especial treat. What he has heretofore produced has, to our humble judgment, oscillated between the laborious and the obscure, and the contemplation of a drama constructed on either principle fails to produce that cheerful and glowing frame of mind which a manager so keenly appreciates in the critic.[2]

Thus there is at least a possibility that O'Brien is the author of these informal reviews, although anything like conclusive evidence is lacking.

Of the hundreds of reviews that Seymour must have written for the Times, only one can definitely be identified as his. Winter, replying to Boucicault's charge that the critics did not have sufficient time to write intelligent reviews, cited a review of "Arrah-na-Pogue" that was written in his presence in forty minutes, and identified Seymour as its author.[3] Since it is the only review known to be

1. 1853, Sept. 15, 4:4 ("The Rivals").
2. 1855, Nov. 22, 4:5 ("Little Treasure").
3. *The Press and the Stage*, p. 43.

by Seymour, it is probably worth quoting in full:

NIBLO'S GARDEN. — Boucicault's spectacular drama of 'Arrah-na-Pogue,' of which we have heard so much, was produced here last evening, and received with favor, warming once or twice into enthusiasm, by an audience that was crowded in every part of the house. The drama is constructed with all Mr. Boucicault's well-known skill, and the dialogue represents that gentleman's and Mr. House's ability in the use of words. The story of the piece is by no means intricate, but we lack time, writing at midnight, to even faintly sketch it. In the main, it is the old Irish legend of the peasant protecting the rebellious and proscribed lord of the soil and nearly getting to the gallows for his pains. In the present case, there is a complication, involving the simple love and troth of *Arrah*, the heroine. She offers the protection of her roof to the McCoul and promises not to divulge the fact for three days. The presence of a stranger in her cottage is discovered by *Michael Feeney*, the informer and villain of the peace [*sic*] and on the day of her wedding to *Shaun*, the post, he divulges the secret, which leads to an uneasy rupture. The best 'sensation' of the play is here. *Shaun* finds his bride overwhelmed with the suspicions of her neighbors, and the accusation of *Feeney* amounting almost to evidence of her guilt. To save her honor he deliberately asserts a falsehood, and says that he was the man who took shelter in her cottage. Hereby he becomes involved in a suppostitious [*sic*] robbery which attaches to the real individual. It is impossible to follow the plot at greater length. It is framed effectively and affords abundant opportunity for stage manager, artist, machinist, and carpenter. The difficulties in the way of production are so many that every allowance ought to be made for a first night. Fortunately, however, allowance was unnecessary. No contretemps occurred. The performance, nevertheless, terminated at a late hour.

We do not regard 'Arrah-na-Pogue' as one of Mr. Boucicault's best productions. It lacks the heartiness of the 'Colleen Bawn,' the contrasts of the 'Octoroon' and the enthusiasm of 'Jessie Brown.' But as Mr. Boucicault can only be judged by himself it may be safely said that it is a better play than any we have had since the production of the pieces we have named. The situations are good, but new only in the way they are wrought. From time immemorial prisoners have escaped by the ivy, which passed the prison window. *Shaun* does the same, and this is the great scene. The stage mechanism is extremely ingenious. The flat sinks as *Shaun* climbs, and so the entire face of the tower passes the eye of the spectator. As an effect, it is one of the best we have ever seen on any stage. Let us add here that the scenery throughout is thoroughly admirable. Some of the landscapes were perfect works of art. Indeed, the entire production of the piece was in the highest degree creditable to Mr. Wheatley.

The cast was good — Mr. Burnett, Mr. E. Sheridan, (a little too vociferous,) Mr. Scallan, (an excellent eccentric comedian,) and Miss Marie

Maeder, being especially worthy of praise. Mr. T. H. Glenny, an artist
new to us, made his first appearance as *Shaun*, and was very warmly
welcomed. He has a good brogue, a portly presence, and a pleasant little
tenor voice. Mr. Glenny was called out at the end of the piece, and,
being unaccountably called on for a speech, made the regulation one on
the part of all the members of the company. The heroine, *Arrah Meelish*,
was impersonated by Miss Josephine Orton, in a graceful and effective
way, but with what was to us a superabundance of whining. The lady
is an experienced and not ungraceful actress. She will improve on ac-
quaintance. Miss Mary Wells, in a small part indeed succeeded, as she
generally does, in making it thoroughly amusing and enjoyable. Her
Barn-door Jig was irresistably comic.

The success of 'Arrah-na-Pogue' was unquestionable. It is destined
to occupy the bills for many weeks.[1]

This review is interesting in several respects. It shows that Winter
tends to be considerably too lenient with his friends and co-pro-
fessionals; time for revision would probably have improved this review to a large extent. The plot of Boucicault's play was evidently
too much for Seymour; no one can read this review and agree that
"the story of the piece is by no means intricate." He made a val-
iant attempt to summarize it, and, after becoming hopelessly tan-
gled, gave it up as a bad job. The review also tends to be incoherent
and diffuse; otherwise, however, it is expert: it covers all the elements of the production, emphasizes the best scenes, compares Boucicault's other plays and appraises the performances of individual
actors. It is, obviously, written in the "sober, business-like" style
of most of the reviews of the period. Finally, the reference to the
"pleasant little tenor voice" betrays the music critic in Seymour; it
indicates perhaps the effects of combining the two tasks in the
same man.

During 1865, Seymour was working for Henry Clapp's New York
Saturday Press; I found four of the columns "Dramatic Feuilletons"
signed "C. B. S.," the signature which Seymour used for his dispatches on the Paris Exposition. In three of these columns, Seymour reviewed plays which had been reviewed in the Times just a
few days earlier. A detailed comparison of excerpts from these reviews may shed some light on the authorship of the Times' reviews
even though it is in at least two cases inconclusive. The first of the
plays was Brougham's "Playing with Fire," reviewed by the Times

1. 1865, July 13, 4:5.

on October 31, 1865,[1] and by the *Saturday Press* on November 4:[2]

Times	Saturday Press
..., Mr. Brougham was — as he stated in his amusing speech — thoroughly bewildered at his reception — which word, we may add, applied to the entire play ... Every scene was applauded, and at the end of each act the fortunate favorite was called out ...	... It was in his own five act comedy and speech that Mr. Brougham made his *rentree*. No one cared a great deal about the former, but the latter filled the house. ... After each act Mr. Brougham was called out. ... With an embarrassment that was delightful he proceeded to make a few remarks. ...
... since Mr. Brougham left there has been no one who could render justice to the part of *Dr. Savage*. The author, to be sure, measured himself for that role. It was considered one of his best fits ...	Mr. Brougham sustained the principal *role* ... with great spirit, and with a healthful gentlemanly bearing which cannot be too highly praised.
... Messrs. Dyott, Walcot and Andrews were also good. ...	Mr. Dyott was excellent as Uncle Timothy, although we failed to perceive the advantage of thickening his voice to a point which sometimes approached mumbling.
The comedy has been placed carefully on the stage, and will undoubtedly enjoy a run.	The Winter Garden Management produced the comedy in a very creditable manner. ...

It is evident that no definite conclusions can be drawn from this comparison. If the Times review is not by Seymour, the comparison merely indicates that both critics liked the play, that both enjoyed Brougham's characterization, that both were struck by the enthusiastic reception, and that both liked Brougham for being embarrassed by it — as any two critics very well might. If Seymour wrote both reviews, then he did not hesitate to express similar opinions, but merely took care to present his material in a different order; and he added — possibly upon reflection — a more detailed criticism of Mr. Dyott. Both conclusions appear to be equally plausible.

The next pair of reviews deals with Palgrave Simpson's "Dreams

1. 5:1.
2. 217:2.

of Delusion," produced at Wallack's. The review in the Times[1]
is written in the conventional manner; that in the *Saturday Press*[2]
is in epistolary form, and consists of brief, staccato, one-sentence
paragraphs. Both state that there is relatively little plot; both summarize whatever plot there is; both note the French play from
which it had been adapted. The Times review stresses an atmos-
phere of tension in the play — "so marked that the cold chills can
be counted" — which Seymour, in the *Saturday Press*, ignores. In
both reviews, however, the remarks on the acting of Frederick
Robinson are strikingly parallel:

Times	*Saturday Press*
The result was due in a great measure to the very quiet, earnest and artistic performances of Mr. Frederick Robinson — a gentleman who has just been added to Mr. Wallack's company.... He is a thor-oughly-experienced actor, whose manner is more French than Eng-lish. He has a good voice and presence; is thoroughly at ease be-fore the audience; avoids super-fluous noise and action, and en-forces his points like a gentle-man....	... his reception was thoroughly cordial ... his voice is good and entirely natural. ... He is either un-acquainted with the art of elocu-tion, or mercifully keeps that knowl-edge to himself ... he came on the stage and left it, like a human be-ing....

The *Saturday Press* review is, of course, considerably more satirical,
but in essence these passages seem to indicate a single author, who
is quite outspokenly opposed to the stagy, hyper-melodramatic
school of acting. Also, the liberal use of the word "thoroughly" is
perhaps supporting evidence that Seymour wrote the Times review
as well as that in the *Saturday Press*.

The third and last pair of reviews,[3] covering the opening of
Lucy Rushton's New York Theatre with "A School for Scandal,"
presents so striking a parallel that Seymour's authorship of the
Times' review can hardly be questioned:

1. 1865, Dec. 13, 4:7.
2. 1865, Dec. 16, 312:1.
3. Times, 1865, Dec. 26, 5:3; New York *Saturday Press*, 1865, Dec. 30, 344:1.

Times	*Saturday Press*
The house was so densely crowded that much personal discomfort prevailed — the rightful owners of seats being deprived of them by hardy invaders, who barely held the policemen in terror.	Miss Rushton's theatre . . . was opened with all the ceremonies of a new police court . . . The possession of a ticket for a reserved seat was regarded as a sufficient proof that the possessor should at once be crushed.
. . . a speech by Miss Rushton . . . was a poetic effusion of whose merits we are unable to speak. Miss Rushton's study of the lines was very imperfect. After clinging desperately to a few cogent rhymes, the lady abandoned the effort and fell back on the ordinary language of the stage.	. . . Miss Rushton made her appearance, and attempted to recite a prologue. The lines escaped her memory, but with ready tact she excused the lapsus, and said 'out of her own head' all that was proper to be said — if not more.
We have never witnessed this witty, but coarse and artificial production, to such eminent disadvantage.	Then came the comedy . . . which, I regret to say, was poorly played.
Mr. Walcot, who portrayed Sir Peter Teazle, was simply ridiculous.	Mr. Walcot's Sir Peter Teazle was a ghastly caricature of the part . . .

As I said, in this pair of reviews the identity of authorship is unmistakeable. The two reviews are parallel not only in the opinions expressed — that in itself would hardly be proof — but also in the degree of satire and violence with which the production is criticized. In addition, these two reviews follow a parallel order of presenting the material.

It is not possible to conclude, however, that Seymour wrote all three Times reviews for which mates appeared in the *Saturday Press*. It is quite possible that he worked for the Times irregularly this year, and thus reviewed a play for both publications as in the case of "A School for Scandal," but reviewed one or both of the others for the *Saturday Press* only. Altogether, this is a regrettably scant collection of Times' reviews which can be assigned to Seymour, considering that the man worked for the Times almost constantly for seventeen years.

The reviews which can be definitely assigned to William Swinton — those of the Rachel performances — have already been discussed in Part II, and there is no other material on him. Nor is there any material whatsoever on the reviews which Daly wrote, other than the vague speculation that he possibly wrote most of the reviews while Seymour was in Paris, from April to about September of 1868.

Most of the material on Schwab's authorship of certain reviews is based, of course, on the New York *Dramatic News*. Untrustworthy though this magazine may be in respect to its opinion of Schwab, its data relating to the authorship problem can, I believe, be considered reliable. Since the *Courier des Etats-Unis* of September 9, 1872, already refers to Schwab as the critic of the Times, it is safe to assume that most of the Times' reviews following that date, and probably those immediately preceding it, were written by Schwab. At the same time, it is known that Schwab travelled occasionally during those years, and it can be assumed that he was on vacation for a number of weeks each year, so that not all of the reviews following that date can be assigned to him. The *Dramatic News* reported Schwab's discharge as drama critic on May 25, 1878; his discharge probably occurred in the week immediately preceding that date. However, Montgomery was hired by the Times sometime in 1877, so that the reviews during that year, and the five months of 1878 preceding Schwab's discharge could be by either Schwab or Montgomery; presumably, they divided the work. Whether Schwab wrote any dramatic reviews after his discharge is doubtful, despite the *Dramatic News'* assertion, since he continued to be employed by the Times.

Definite identification of his authorship can be made only in connection with two reviews, still only on the basis of the *Dramatic News*. Both reviews are probably worth quoting here; the first joins with the rest of the New York press in condemning C. J. Smith's "The Flatterer":

TWENTY-THIRD STREET THEATRE

The beautiful little theatre until lately known as Darling's Opera House was last evening opened to the public as a dramatic resort, where comedies and dramas of a lighter type than are usually presented may be witnessed. The company which has been brought together, includes some well-known artists, such as Messrs. Jennings, Lingham, and Vandenhoff and Mmes. Deland and Sara Stevens, and the *mise en scene* shown yesterday was fresh and elegant. But all the possibilities of the theatre and the actors went for nothing on account of the piece. There is, indeed, a plot in 'The Flatterer,' but it is so terribly complicated that an insight into its intricacies is almost unobtainable. When we add that the development of the story is of the feeblest, that the characters are trivial and ill-drawn, and that the dialogue is commonplace and pointless we need offer no apology for not entering into details as to the new play. It was bad enough to be set down as a perfect failure, and more it is unnecessary to say. Yesterday's audience was bored, but 'The Flatterer' being harmless in its worthlessness, no demonstration of displeasure occurred. With an interesting drama or comedy, the chances of life of the Twenty-Third Street Theatre would be good; its present prospects, with 'The Flatterer' as the intended attraction, are far from bright.[1]

The other review concerned Anna Dickinson's "A Crown of Thorns," and demonstrates the same acerbity as the review of "The Flatterer," as well as the same choice of strong, poignant figures of speech.

> . . . The piece . . . is written . . . in a manner indicating the author's total blindness to the dramatic art. 'A Crown of Thorns' has not undergone any perceptible modification since it was first brought out, and Miss Dickinson, as an actress, has not changed materially. Last night she appeared somewhat more at ease on the stage than when she first trod the boards a twelvemonth ago, but something of the little fire and force then observable at intervals seems to have vanished. Miss Dickinson at present is simply an intelligent and ambitious woman who knows exactly how feeling and passion ought to be depicted for the edification of the public, but is debarred by nature and ignorance from the gifts and acquirements needed for their illustration. She has neither voice, nor commanding figure, nor expressive features, nor power of gesture. Her anger is mere pettishness, her pride vexation and her vengeance spitefulness . . . Miss Dickinson, as an actress and dramatist, has not the slightest claim on public attention. Although the general performance last evening was far from good, the labors of the humblest 'utility man' would in justice merit more consideration than those of the leading personage. . .[2]

The review printed in the Times of the earlier performance of this play under the title "Ann Boleyn," in Boston,[3] is sufficiently similar to this one to support the supposition that Schwab had seen and reviewed the Boston production, and, upon seeing its revival in New York, may have rushed out after the first act, as the *Dramatic News* charges, because he was convinced that there had been no substantial change.

No other of the Times' reviews could be identified as Schwab's.

Montgomery, as I said before, joined the Times in 1877; he probably wrote at least some of the criticism for the Times during that

1. 1875, Dec. 14, 4:6.
2. 1877, Apr. 5, 5:2.
3. 1876, May 9, 7:1.

year and during the early part of 1878, and apparently wrote most
of the reviews after Schwab was discharged, in May of that year.
Again, not all the reviews during that period can be positively assigned to him, since he, too, must have had substitutes while he
was on vacation or on other assignments. His authorship of three
reviews is definitely established by the *Dramatic News*. The first
of these, treating a performance of Frederick Marsden's "Otto, a
German," at the Broadway,[1] was roundly condemned by the
Dramatic News as "twaddle," since it allegedly gave the star, George
S. Knight, credit for being a good comedian, a talented dancer, and
altogether a "hit," while it at the same time tried to belittle his performance and his contribution to the play as a whole. Actually,
this criticism is not fair. The review is certainly incoherent, and at
times even confused; but Montgomery did make his point, which
the *Dramatic News* obviously missed: the play was nothing but a
collection of ill-assorted variety sketches which made insufficient
use of Knight's talents, so that his performance was poor despite
his capabilities. Montgomery listed the few scenes in which Knight
was able to display his special talents, and continued: "As he has
little to do, therefore, save to act — to appear at the critical junc-
ture of the story, and to thwart the villain — he soon becomes
tiresome . . ." The *Dramatic News* deliberately misinterpreted
Montgomery's use of the word "act," and questioned what else a
comedian was supposed to do; obviously, however, Montgomery
used the word, perhaps unfortunately, in the sense of advancing
the plot, and thus, of course, his criticism is not at all contradictory.[2]

The other two reviews concern the same play, Cazauran's "Lost
Children," which was performed at the Union Square Theatre on
April 17, 1879. The *Dramatic News* charged that Montgomery's
statement about the play in a summary at the end of the season[3]
directly contradicted his full-length critique after the premiere.[4]
Careful examination of both articles shows that the charge was
completely unfounded. The full-length review was devoted largely
to a vigorous condemnation of the admitted plagiarism in the play;
Montgomery pointed out not only the sources from which the plot

---

1. 1878, Nov. 5, 4:7.
2. This tends to confirm my opinion that the *Dramatic News* sank, on occasion, to
the level of a completely untrustworthy, malicious scandal-sheet; and it is possible that it
transferred its animosity toward Schwab to his successor on the Times.
3. June 1, 2:5.
4. Apr. 18, 5:1.

and the characters were taken, but also the devastating effect on the younger playwrights of the day which such practices might have. He referred to the problem again in his summary at the end of the season. In both the review and the summary, he noted that the play showed that its author had "a deft hand at playwriting," and that the play had "plenty of romantic interest." In the review, he mentioned that the "story is . . . unraveled with . . . ingenuity," and that the acting was satisfactory; these points did not appear in the summary. The summary, on the other hand, contained some generalities not brought out in the original review; apparently Montgomery thought that the details in the full-length review conveyed the general impression adequately, with no need for a resume. Altogether, there are no differences between the review and the summary that cannot be simply accounted for by the fact that the review occupied an entire column, while the summary was a three-line, one-sentence statement.

Montgomery's background — as little of it as is known — seems certainly to indicate that he is the author of the reviews of the Shakespearean performances which I have already discussed at length; however, no further positive identification could be made.

The scarcity of the material about the critics and their relations to the Times reviews is worse than unfortunate. Even though the influence of the dramatic reviews in the daily press on the theatre and on the public, both in the period under study and today, cannot be accurately measured, it can be readily discerned. Especially the more militant critiques and editorials of the late sixties and seventies seem to indicate, by their very content, that they not only echo theatrical trends, but shape them as well. Those who are interested in these trends must almost necessarily regret the lack of information about the men who, through their daily reviews in the newspapers, played their part in shaping them. O'Brien, Seymour, Schwab, Montgomery are now merely nebulous figures in the history of the Times and of the New York stage; more information about their personal background would undoubtedly add to our knowledge of both contemporary journalism and the contemporary theatre.

Then there are questions about the Times' critics as individuals. What is the relation, if any, between O'Brien's hack work for the Times, and his other writings? What, if anything, is true about the charges of Schwab's corruption? And, probably most important of all, what effect did Daly's work for the Times have on his later

career in the theatre?   What precisely was Leland's work for the
Times, or Hurlbert's?

The value of information constituting answers to these and similar questions can hardly be overemphasized.   These critics were
experts who guided, to an undoubtedly considerable extent, a
large part of the daily theatre audience.   Their reviews are expert
reports.   They were probably not deserving of the blind praise
that Winter bestowed on the profession; they evidently made mis-
takes.   But neither were they deserving of the blind condemnation
by such men as Boucicault or Burton or the "Town Crier" in the
New York *Dramatic News* or the editors of *The Round Table*.   Nor
were they deserving, it seems to me, of the all but total obscurity
which hides them now.

BIBLIOGRAPHY

Clipping files, New York Public Library, Theatre Collection.

Scrapbook on Augustin Daly, Museum of the City of New York, Theatre Library.

Scrapbooks, Robinson Locke Collection, New York Public Library.

Scrapbooks, Stead Collection, New York Public Library.

Appleton's Cyclopedia of American Biography, New York, D. Appleton & Co., 1900.

Brother Jonathan (New York).

New York *Clipper.*

The Critic (New York).

Dictionary of American Biography, New York, Charles Scribner's Sons, 1936.

New York *Dramatic Mirror.*

New York *Dramatic News.*

Harper's Weekly.

Kleine Musik-Zeitung (New York).

The Literary World; A Journal of Science, Literature and Art (New York).

Memories of Daly's Theatres, privately printed, 1897 (copyright by Augustin Daly, 1896).

National Cyclopedia of American Biography, New York, James T. White & Co., 1897.

The Round Table, A Weekly Record of the Notable, the Useful and the Tasteful (New York).

New York *Saturday Press.*

New York *Times.*

New York *Times,* Jubilee Supplement, September 18, 1901 (issued September 25).

New York *Times,* Supplement, "Twenty-Five Years of the New-

York Times," September 88,1876.

Who Was Who in America, Chicago, The A. N. Marquis Co., 1942.

Aldrich, (Mrs.) Thomas Bailey, *Crowding Memories,* New York, Houghton Mifflin Co., 1920.

Alger, William Rounseville, *Life of Edwin Forrest,* Philadelphia, J. B. Lippincott & Co., 1877.

Bacon, Edgar Mayhew, "J.P.M., Personal Reminiscences of the Author of 'A Journey to Nature,' etc.," *The World's Work,* New York, Doubleday, Page & Co., 1903, Vol. VI, p. 3477.

Barrus, Clara, *Whitman and Burroughs, Comrades,* Boston, Houghton Mifflin Co., 1931.

Beers, Henry Putney, *Bibliographies in American History,* New York, The H. W. Wilson Co., 1932.

Binns, Henry Bryan, *A Life of Walt Whitman,* London, Methuen & Co., 1905.

Bodeen, DeWitt, "Adelaide Neilson of the Midnight Eye," *Pasadena (California) Playhouse News,* June 15, 1936, p.4.

Bond, F. Fraser, *Mr. Miller of "The Times," The Story of an Editor,* New York, Charles Scribner's Sons, 1931.

Boucicault, Dion, "At the Goethe Society" (an address), *North American Review,* Vol. CXLVIII, No. 338, p. 335 (March, 1889).

Bradley, Edward Sculley, *George Henry Boker, Poet and Patriot,* Philadelphia, University of Pennsylvania Press, 1927.

Brawley, Benjamin, *A Short History of the English Drama,* New York, Harcourt, Brace & Co., 1921.

Brockway, Beman, *Fifty Years in Journalism, Embracing Recollections and Personal Experiences,* Watertown, New York, Daily Times Printing & Publishing House, 1891.

Brooks, Van Wyck, *Sketches in Criticism,* New York, E. P. Dutton & Co., 1932.

Brown, John Mason, *Upstage,* New York, W. W. Norton & Co., Inc., 1930.

Brown, Thomas Allston, *History of the American Stage,* New York, Dick & Fitzgerald, 1870.

Brown, Thomas Allston, *A History of the New York Stage,* New

York, Dodd, Mead & Co., 1903.

Clapp, Henry Austin, *Reminiscences of a Dramatic Critic,* New York, Houghton Mifflin Co., 1902.

Clarke, Asia Booth, *The Elder and the Younger Booth,* Boston, James R. Osgood & Co., 1882.

Clement, Clara Erskine, *Charlotte Cushman,* Boston, James R. Osgood & Co., 1882.

Copeland, Charles Townsend, *Edwin Booth,* Boston, Small, Maynard & Co., 1901.

Daly, Augustin, "The American Dramatist," *North American Review,* Vol. CXLII, p. 485.

Daly, Joseph Francis, *The Life of Augustin Daly,* New York, The Macmillan Co., 1917.

Danielson, Henry, *Bibliographies of Modern Authors,* London, The Bookman's Journal, 1921.

Davis, Elmer Holmes, *History of the New York Times (1851-1921),* New York, The New York Times Co., 1921.

Debs, Eugene Victor, *John Swinton: Radical Editor and Leader,* Berkeley Heights, New Jersey, The Oriole Press, 1939.

DeCasseres, Benjamin, *James Gibbons Huneker,* New York, Joseph Lawren, 1925.

DeLeon, Thomas Cooper, *Belles, Beaux and Brains of the Sixties,* New York, G. W. Dillingham Co., 1907.

DeMille, George E., *Literary Criticism in America,* New York, The Dial Press, 1931.

Derby, J. C., *Fifty Years Among Authors, Books and Publishers,* New York, G. W. Carleton & Co., 1884.

Deutsch, Babette, *Walt Whitman, Builder for America,* New York, Julian Messner, Inc., 1941.

Douglas, Paul H., *Real Wages in the United States,* 1890-1926, New York, Houghton Mifflin Co., 1930.

Drew, (Mrs.) John, *Autobiographical Sketch,* New York, Charles Scribner's Sons, 1899.

Elderkin, John, *A Brief History of the Lotos Club,* (copyright by the Lotos Club), New York, Press of MacGowan & Slipper, 1895.

Evans, Frederick, "Noah Brooks," *The Lamp, A Review and Record of Current Literature,* Vol. XXVII, p. 128 (September, 1903).

Evans, T. C., "William Henry Hurlbert," New York *Times* Saturday Supplement, 1902, June 14, 1:1.

Eytinge, Rose, *The Memories of Rose Eytinge,* New York, Frederick A. Stokes Co., 1905.

Fairbanks, Charles Bullard (?), *My Unknown Chum "Aguecheek,"* New York, Devin-Adair Co., 1912 (1917) [*sic*].

Fatout, Paul, "An Enchanted Titan," *South Atlantic Quarterly,* Vol. XXX, p. 51 (1931).

Foerster, Norman, *American Criticism,* New York, Houghton Mifflin Co., 1928.

Ford, Edwin H., *A Bibliography of Literary Journalism in America,* Minneapolis, Burgess Publishing Co., 1937.

Ford, Edwin H., *History of Journalism in the United States* (A Bibliography), Minneapolis, Burgess Publishing Co., 1938.

Ford, James L., *Forty-Odd Years in the Literary Shop,* New York, E. P. Dutton & Co., 1921.

Freedley, George, and Reeves, John A., *A History of the Theatre,* New York, Crown Publishers, 1941.

Glicksberg, Charles I., "Charles Godfrey Leland and 'Vanity Fair,' " *Pennsylvania Magazine,* Vol. LXII, No. 3, p. 309 (July, 1938).

Greenslet, Ferris, *The Life of Thomas Bailey Aldrich,* New York, Houghton Mifflin Co., 1908.

Hale, E. E., "Wealth and Beauty. A Poem; read before the Phi Beta Kappa Society, in Cambridge, July 19, 1855. By William Henry Hurlbert," *North American Review,* Vol. LXXXI, p. 546 (October, 1855).

Hall, Margaret, "Personal Recollections of Augustin Daly," *The Theatre,* Vol. V, No. 52, p. 150; No. 53, p. 174; No. 54, p. 188; No. 55, p. 213 (1905).

Harrison, Gabriel, *Edwin Forrest, The Actor and the Man,* New York, privately published), 1889.

Hillyer, William Sidney, a memorial article on Fitz-James O'Brien (untitled), New York *Times* Saturday Review of Books and Art, 1898, July 2, 445:2.

Holloway, Emory, and Schwarz, Vernolian (eds.), *I Sit and Look Out, Editorials from the Brooklyn Daily Times,* by Walt Whitman, New York, Columbia University Press, 1932.

Holloway, Laura C. (Mrs. Langford), *Adelaide Neilson, A Souvenir,* New York, Funk & Wagnalls, 1885.

Howells, William Dean, *Literary Friends and Acquaintances,* New York, Harper & Brothers, 1900.

Huneker, James Gibbons, *Essays,* New York, Charles Scribner's Sons, 1929.

Huneker, James Gibbons, *Ivory Apes and Peacocks,* New York, Charles Scribner's Sons, 1915.

Huneker, James Gibbons, *Old Fogy,* Philadelphia, Theodore Presser Co., 1913.

Huneker, James Gibbons, *Steeplejack,* New York, Charles Scribner's Sons, 1915.

Huneker, Josephine (ed.), *Intimate Letters of James Gibbons Huneker,* New York, Boni & Liveright, 1924.

Huneker, Josephine (ed.), *Letters of James Gibbons Huneker,* New York, Charles Scribner's Sons, 1922.

Hurlbutt, Henry H., *The Hurlbut Genealogy,* Albany, Joel Munsell's Sons, 1888.

Hutton, Laurence (ed.), *Opening Addresses,* New York, The Dunlap Society, 1887.

Ireland, Joseph N., *Records of the New York Stage from 1750 to 1860,* New York, T. H. Morrell, 1867.

Jefferson, Eugenie Paul, *Intimate Recollections of Joseph Jefferson,* New York, Dodd, Mead & Co., 1909.

Jefferson, Joseph, *The Autobiography of Joseph Jefferson,* New York, The Century Co., 1890.

Jenkins, Stephen, *The Greatest Street in the World,* New York, G. P. Putnam's Sons, 1911.

Kimmel, Stanley, *The Mad Booths of Maryland,* New York, Bobbs-Merrill Co., 1940.

Krows, Arthur Edwin, "Adolph Klauber [New York *Times*] on Appreciative Criticism," New York *Dramatic Mirror,* Vol. LXXI, 1914, Feb. 18, p. 3.

Krows, Arthur Edwin, "Arthur Ruhl [New York *Tribune*] at the Critics' Round Table," New York *Dramatic Mirror,* Vol. LXXI, 1914, Feb. 18, p. 3.

Krows, Arthur Edwin, "Burns Mantle [New York *Evening Mail*] Separates Critics from Critics," New York *Dramatic Mirror,* Vol. LXXI, 1914, March 4, p. 3.

Kuznets, Simon, *National Income,* New York, National Bureau of Economic Research, 1946.

Lancaster, Albert Edmund, *All's Dross But Love,* New York, John W. Lovell Co., 1889.

Lancaster, Albert Edmund, and Vincent, Frank, *The Lady of Cawnpore,* New York, Funk & Wagnalls, 1891.

Leavitt, M. B., *Fifty Years in Theatrical Management* (1859-1909), New York, Broadway Publishing Co., 1912.

Lee, James Melvin, *History of American Journalism,* Boston, Houghton Mifflin Co., 1917.

Leland, Charles Godfrey, *Memoirs,* London, William Heinemann, 1891.

Lockridge, Richard, *Darling of Misfortune: Edwin Booth, 1833-1893,* New York, The Centure Co., 1932.

Malvern, Gladys, *Good Troopers All, The Story of Joseph Jefferson,* Philadelphia, MacRae, Smith & Co., 1945.

Matthews, Brander, and Hutton, Laurence (eds.), *Actors and Actresses of Great Britain and the United States,* New York, Cassell & Co., Ltd., 1886.

Matthews, Brander, *Americanisms and Briticisms with other Essays on other isms,* New York, Harper & Brothers, 1892.

Matthews, Brander, *A Book About the Theatre,* New York, Charles Scribner's Sons, 1916.

Matthews, Brander, *Playwrights on Playmaking and other Studies of the Stage,* New York, Charles Scribner's Sons, 1923.

Matthews, Brander, *These Many Years,* New York, Charles Scribner's Sons, 1917.

Maverick, Augustus, *Henry J. Raymond and the New York Press for Thirty Years (1840-1870),* Hartford, Connecticut, A. S. Hale & Co., 1870.

Mitchell, Edward P., *Memoirs of an Editor*, New York, Charles Scribner's Sons, 1924.

Montgomery, George Edgar (ed.), *Sidney Woollett*, Newport, Rhode Island, Daily News Print, 1890.

Moses, Montrose Jonas, *The American Dramatist*, Boston, Little, Brown & Co., 1925.

Moses, Montrose Jonas, and Brown, John Mason (eds.), *The American Theatre as Seen by its Critics, 1752-1934*, New York, W. W. Norton & Co., Inc., 1934.

Moses, Montrose Jonas, *Famous Actor-Families in America*, New York, Thomas Y. Crowell & Co., 1906.

Mott, Frank Luther, *American Journalism, A History of Newspapers in the United States through 250 Years, 1690-1940*, New York, The Macmillan Co., 1942.

Nathan, George Jean, *The Critic and the Drama*, New York, Alfred A. Knopf, 1922.

Nevins, Allan, *The Evening Post*, New York, Boni & Liveright, 1922.

Nichols, Lewis, "The Nine Gold Men of Broadway," The New York *Times* Magazine, 1947, Nov. 16, p. 17.

O'Brien, Edward J. (ed.), *The Collected Stories of Fitz-James O'Brien*, New York, Albert & Charles Boni, 1925.

O'Brien, Frank M., *The Story of the Sun*, New York, D. Appleton & Co., 1928.

Odell, George Clinton Densmore, *Annals of the New York Stage*, New York, Columbia University Press, 1927-1945.

Parry, Albert, *Garrets and Pretenders, A History of Bohemianism in America*, New York, Covici Friede Publishers, 1933.

Pattee, Fred Lewis, *The Development of the American Short Story*, New York, Harper & Brothers, 1923.

Pennell, Elizabeth Robins, "A Bundle of Old Letters," *Atlantic Monthly*, Vol. XCV, p. 309.

Pennell, Elizabeth Robins, *Charles Godfrey Leland*, New York, Houghton Mifflin Co., 1906.

Pennell, Elizabeth Robins, "Hans Breitmann," *Atlantic Monthly*, Vol. XCV, p. 73.

Pennell, Elizabeth Robins, "Hans Breitmann as Romany Rye," *Atlantic Monthly,* Vol. XCV, p. 154.

Price, William Thompson, *A Life of Charlotte Cushman,* New York, Brentano's 1894.

Quinn, Arthur Hobson, *The American Drama From the Civil War to the Present Day,* New York, F. S. Crofts & Co., 1937.

Rees, James (Colley Cibber), *The Life of Edwin Forrest with Reminiscences and Personal Recollections,* Philadelphia, T. B. Peterson & Brothers, 1874.

Reilly, Joseph J., "A Keltic Poe," *The Catholic World,* Vol. CX, p. 751 (1920).

Robins, Edward, "Random Recollections of 'Hans Breitmann,' " *Pennsylvania Magazine,* Vol. XLIX, p. 141 (1925).

Rogers, Cameron, *The Magnificent Idler, The Story of Walt Whitman,* Garden City, New York, Doubleday, Page & Co., 1926.

Russell, W. Clark, *Representative Actors,* New York, Frederick Warne & Co., 1888.

Seymour, Charles C. Bailey, *Self-Made Men,* New York, Harper & Brothers, 1858.

Sherwood, (Mrs.) M. E. W., "Fitzjames O'Brien," New York *Times* Saturday Review of Books and Art, 1898, July 2, 444:2.

Smith, Bernard, *Forces in American Criticism,* New York, Harcourt, Brace & Co., 1939.

Stebbins, Emma (ed.), *Charlotte Cushmann, Her Letters and Memories of Her Life,* Boston, Houghton, Osgood & Co., The Riverside Press, Cambridge [*sic*], 1879.

Stedman, Laura, and Gould, George Milbry, *Life and Letters of Edmund Clarence Stedman,* New York, Moffat, Yard & Co., 1910.

Stoddard, Richard Henry, "The Best of the Bohemians," *The Critic,* Vol. I, p. 44 (1881).

Stone, Henry Dickinson, *Personal Recollections of the Drama or Theatrical Reminiscences, etc.,* Albany, New York, Charles Van Benthuysen & Sons, 1873.

Sweeney, John F., *A Study of the New York Times,* Cleveland, J. F. Sweeney, 1922.

New York *Times, The Seventy-Fifth Anniversary of the New York Times,* New York, The New York Times Co., 1926.

Towse, John Ranken, *Sixty Years of the Theatre,* New York, Funk & Wagnalls, 1916.

Traubel, Horace, *With Walt Whitman in Camden,* Boston, Small, Maynard & Co., 1906.

United States Department of Labor, Bureau of Labor Statistics, *Bulletin No. 604,* "History of Wages in the United States from Colonial Times to 1928," Part II.

Waters, Robert, *Career and Conversation of John Swinton,* Chicago, Charles H. Kerr & Co., 1902.

Whitman, Walt, *A Child's Reminiscence,* Seattle, University of Washington Bookstore [*sic*], 1930.

Whitman, Walt, manuscript letters in the Berg Collection, New York Public Library.

Wilson, Francis, *Joseph Jefferson, Reminiscences of a Fellow Player,* New York, Charles Scribner's Sons, 1906.

Wilstach, Frank, scrapbook, Theatre Collection, New York Public Library.

Winter, William, *The Actor and Other Speeches,* New York, The Dunlap Society, 1891.

Winter, William, *Brief Chronicles,* New York, The Dunlap Society, 1889.

Winter, William, *Brown Heath and Blue Bells, with Other Papers,* New York, Macmillan & Co., 1895.

Winter, William, *The Life and Art of Edwin Booth,* New York, Macmillan & Co., 1893.

Winter, William, *The Life and Art of Joseph Jefferson,* New York, Macmillan & Co., 1894.

Winter, William, *The Life of David Belasco,* New York, Moffat, Yard & Co., 1918.

Winter, William (ed.), *The Life, Stories and Poems of John Brougham,* Boston, James R. Osgood & Co., 1881.

Winter, William, *Old Friends, Being Literary Recollections of Other Days,* New York, Moffat, Yard & Co., 1909.

Winter, William, *Other Days, Being Chronicles and Memories of the Stage,* New York, Moffat, Yard & Co., 1908.

Winter, William (ed.), *The Poems and Stories of Fitz-James O'Brien,* Boston, James R. Osgood & Co., 1881.

Winter, William, *The Press and the Stage,* An Oration Delivered Before the Goethe Society at the Brunswick Hotel, New York on January 28, 1889, New York, Lockwood & Coombes, 1889.

Winter, William, *Shadows of the Stage,* New York, The Macmillan Co., 1906.

Winter, William, *Vagrant Memories, Being Further Recollections of Other Days,* New York, George H. Doran Co., 1915.

Winter, William, *The Wallet of Times, Containing Personal, Biographical, and Critical Reminiscences of the American Theatre,* New York, Moffat, Yard & Co., 1913.

Winter, William, *A Wreath of Laurel,* New York, The Dunlap Society, 1898.

Wolle, Francis, "Fitz-James O'Brien," *University of Colorado Studies,* Series B, Studies in the Humanities, Vol. II, No. 2, Boulder, Colorado, University of Colorado Press, 1944.